GETTING STARTED IN
EGG DECORATION

Books in the *Getting Started* series

African Crafts

Batik

Building Model Airplanes

Candlemaking

Ceramics

Dried Flower Craft

Egg Decoration

Handmade Rugs

Kitemaking

Leathercraft

Macramé

Mineral Collecting

Plastics

Prints and Patterns

Silk Screening

Tie-Dyeing

Weaving

GETTING STARTED IN
EGG DECORATION

NANCY M. LANG

The Bruce Publishing Company / New York

Collier–Macmillan Limited / London

Library of Congress Catalog Card Number: 78-160383

THE BRUCE PUBLISHING COMPANY
866 THIRD AVENUE, NEW YORK, NEW YORK 10022

COLLIER-MACMILLAN CANADA, LTD., TORONTO, ONTARIO

Made in the United States of America

CONTENTS

ACKNOWLEDGMENTS

I wish to thank my husband, Ronald Lang, who has done most of the photography, and whose help and advice has been invaluable.

My thanks also to Mrs. F. R. Lawson and Mrs. Mary Sammartino who have shared their techniques and contributed photographs of their eggs, and to Edith Walker who shared her secret of the porcelain finish.

Credit should be given to C. Jack DeLoach and Gordon Moore, both of Columbia, Missouri, who took, respectively, the black-and-white photographs and the color slides of Mrs. Lawson's eggs; and to Mr. Harold C. Lang, Jr. for the photograph in Plate 16.

Much of the photoprocessing was done by Winant Brothers, Inc., of Baltimore, Maryland. Except where noted, all the eggs were decorated by the author.

INTRODUCTION

Decorated eggs are presently enjoying renewed popularity with collectors and hobbyists. Beautifully painted and jewelled eggs appear frequently in public displays and magazine illustrations. Handcrafted ones are often sold in large department stores and specialty shops. In this book you will learn how these lovely ornaments can be created easily at home with inexpensive materials and used, for example, as delightful bazaar items, Christmas tree ornaments, and gifts. The book also gives detailed directions for producing the elegant jewelled eggs that are becoming so popular.

Painting eggs at Easter is an ancient custom. Since the time of the Egyptians, eggs have been symbolic of rebirth and fertility. They represented renewal of life for the early Persians, Greeks, and Hindus, and Christians eventually assimilated the egg into their Easter celebration.

As early as the thirteenth century, eggshells were painted with religious illustrations. In the sixteenth century Francis I of France was given an eggshell which contained a wood carving of the passion of Christ. Both Louis XIV and Louis XV received painted eggshells on Easter mornings. Watteau, Boucher, and Lancret are among those artists said to have painted such eggs, and the styles they created can be imitated today. At Easter the

Russian aristocracy traditionally exchanged porcelain or cloisonné eggs that contained an icon or small gift.

Inspired by this long tradition of egg decorating, Peter Carl Fabergé made Easter eggs of precious metals which were given to the empress and dowager empress of Russia in the years before the 1917 revolution. These exquisite eggs, many of which are still in existence, marked the high point of the craft. They were elaborately trimmed and contained lids and doors that opened to reveal beautifully crafted surprises inside.

Some of Fabergé's eggs can be seen in museum collections; others are in private collections. There are excellent books available on Fabergé which include color illustrations of his eggs. This material is an inspiration to the contemporary craftsman working with real eggshells.

Egg decoration is also an important element of folk art. The Central Europeans use wax and natural dyes to create intricate designs on real eggshells. They use the symbols typical of their art: triangles, stars, the sun, chickens, deer, fir trees, and flowers. Their work has great appeal today and is easily reproduced (Plate 7).

There are almost as many ways to decorate eggs as there are hobbyists. One can find inspiration in the elaborately gilded and jewelled eggs of Imperial Russia and France or in the delightful folk arts of many cultures. Contemporary ideas are illustrated here and in popular magazines at Christmas and Easter. Most exciting of all, the egg can become a part of the unique experience of the individual craftsman who works with it. It is in the hands of the craftsman that it offers its greatest possibilities for creativity.

When planning his own designs, the beginner should be aware of the many designs around him. Fabric patterns, magazine illustrations, advertisements, Christmas cards, and gift-wrap paper have all been planned by professional artists and offer the hobbyist a do-it-yourself course in design. Save and copy the best of these designs.

This book is designed to provide a springboard for the reader's own ideas and innovations. He will want to experiment with combinations of finishes, trims, and designs; make improvements on them; and add new methods of his own. Whatever techniques the hobbyist uses, the style he develops will be unique.

Egg craft can be as inexpensive as the hobbyist wishes. At the same time, it offers the craftsman free rein for his talents and imagination. The egg itself is as close as the refrigerator. It can be trimmed with a variety of items found around the house. Indeed, finding new uses for old discarded pieces of jewelry and fabric is one of the delights of egg craft.

Hand-decorated eggs make exciting bazaar items. Many simple ideas are included in the sections on painted and covered eggs. For example, trim a dozen hens' eggs in different colors, and display them in the original egg carton.

Eggs make wonderfully individual gifts for the person who has everything. Try giving a set of hens' eggs painted as Christmas tree ornaments or a single, exquisitely jewelled window egg containing a Christmas scene. One might give an egg that has been made into a box to hold a ring, or a housewarming egg done in the colors of the new home. A window egg holding a tiny picture of a graduation or wedding will become a treasured memento.

The hobbyist can use his eggs as a decorative motif throughout his home. He might fill a huge brandy snifter with them; make them into a mobile; hang them on his Christmas tree; or exhibit them in their own glass case. They may be displayed in an Easter basket or in a large, abandoned bird's nest. (If an authentic bird's nest is used, it should be sprayed with insecticide.)

At Easter an egg tree can be made by placing a leafless tree branch in a vase. The branch can be spray-painted or left natural. The vase must have a bottom large enough to be stable. Fill it with sand and anchor the branch securely in the packed sand. Then hang the eggs with wire Christmas ornament hangers. Group standing eggs around the completed egg tree.

A mobile of eggs can be constructed with lengths of coat-hanger wire and clear nylon cord. The eggs are hung with loops of nylon line and they can be weighted with sand or lead shot to provide balance.

A small table with a recessed glass top or a glass-fronted shadow box makes an excellent permanent display for eggs. Cup shelves and breakfronts also make handsome egg cabinets. Eggs are particularly effective when grouped in front of, or standing on, a mirror.

Small wood or plexiglass cubes make convenient stands for eggs. An ornate egg decorated in an Imperial or Victorian tradition may be housed under a glass bell dome. The decorative stands that are sold in rock shops to hold mineral samples make very nice egg stands.

Getting Started in Egg Decoration outlines instructions for a variety of approaches to egg decorating. These methods can be combined or used individually. The overall style of the individual egg should be considered when combining techniques because some are more suitable for combination than others.

Whether you keep your own eggs, sell them, or give them as gifts, you should inscribe them with your initials or some identifying sign in an inconspicuous spot in the design. Who knows but that today's hobby may provide tomorrow's heirlooms?

1
BASIC SUPPLIES
AND PROCEDURES

No matter how you plan to decorate your eggs — simply or elaborately — it is important that you gather your basic supplies and equipment first. Then review the fundamental procedures involved so that you have a firm foundation on which to begin your work in egg craft.

SUPPLIES AND EQUIPMENT

Cotton swabs help to clean excess glue from the eggs as you work.

Fingernail polish remover can be used to clean off Duco cement.

Forceps are needed to apply trims.

Glue, cement (Duco), in addition to its many other incidental uses, is used to apply decorations and to repair and harden shells. White glue is used both for applying trims and in some finishes. If you buy it in pint or half-pint quantities, pour a small amount into a small glass jar with a tight-fitting lid which will be easier to keep clean than the original container. The lid and rim of the jar should be washed regularly to prevent sticking. Before it dries, white glue can be washed out of brushes with water.

Kneading erasers are useful for picking up small jewels and sequins one at a time. The eraser is placed on the end of a toothpick and is an invaluable tool when doing any amount of jewelling or beading. The other end of the toothpick can be used to nudge the jewel into place. From time to time remove the eraser and reknead it. A large piece of eraser will remove fingerprints and pencil marks from finished eggs.

Needles are used to pierce the shell in order to empty the egg.

Paint brushes (½ inch and ¼ inch, Sizes 1 and 000) will be necessary. Save any old brushes for spreading glue, cement, and wax. Follow the directions on the paint container for cleaning brushes.

Paints, trims, and decorations are your most important supplies. These will serve as your inspiration. Purchase them in the smallest quantities available, but accumulate a large selection. Part of the fun in egg decorating is finding new uses for familiar items. Have a box in which to keep leftover trim and "found" objects from the store or the attic. Empty egg cartons and plastic ice-cube trays are handy for storing beads and trims.

Paper towels protect unfinished eggs from accidental marring and moisture from the hands.

A **rack** for drying painted eggs is almost essential and can be made easily at home. Drive several long finishing nails through a board, spacing them 2 to 3 inches apart so that the eggs will not touch. Slip the eggs over the nails to hang until dry. To make a rack for larger goose eggs, pound "starter" holes partway through the board with a long nail. Space these 3 or 4 inches apart. Cut a painted wire coat hanger into 4-inch pieces and hammer them into the starter holes. A drop of glue in the hole at the base of each wire will stabilize it.

Razor blades are used to cut the shell.

Scissors are needed to cut and trim decorations and shells.

Toothbrushes are useful for scouring shells and removing membrane.

Toothpicks are needed to apply trims and spread glue.

Wax, jeweler's, mounted on a toothpick or a hatpin, can be used in the same ways as the eraser to handle very small jewels.

SOURCES OF EGGS

Egg decorating need not be confined to hens' eggs. Eggs range in size from small bantam eggs to large goose eggs. The goose eggs are very desirable because of their size, shape, and strength, but they can be difficult to find. Duck, turkey, and goose hatcheries will often sell eggs which have failed to hatch. These can be located through farmers' markets and wholesale poultry dealers. Some mail-order houses periodically advertise goose eggs. A rural livestock supply store can sometimes refer you to someone who raises fowl and sells extra eggs. Bantam and pullet eggs are readily available in season from farmers, as are small and extra-large hens' eggs. Zoos occasionally have a surplus of various eggs which have failed to hatch.

Wild bird eggs should never be used because the parent birds will abandon the nest once the eggs are gone. Ostrich eggs can occasionally be purchased, but their use encourages collectors to continue to rob nests and thus threaten the birds with extinction.

It is important to keep in mind also that there are federal and state laws which impose penalties for taking eggs, or even touching the nests, of any wild birds at any time of the year. For permission to approach wild birds' nests for research, both state and federal permits must be acquired and even these are very rarely granted.

CLEANING EGGS

The first step in decorating the egg is to clean the shell and remove the contents. (Egg dyeing is an exception to this rule, for the egg should be dyed before the contents are removed.) Shells that are cut in half or have a window are emptied when they are cut. If the shell is to remain whole, the contents must be forced out of a hole in one end. To do this, make a small hole in each end of the shell with a darning needle, and gently blow into one end, forcing the contents out of the other.

Occasionally eggs will have been left in an incubator until it becomes obvious that they will not hatch. To clean spoiled eggs such as these might be, insert a long needle into the egg and scramble the contents. Enlarge the hole slightly at one end and shake out the egg, or hold it under cold water until it is flushed clean. A turkey baster, an old syringe, or a football pump can be used to force air into one end of an egg and drive the contents out of the opposite hole. A hypodermic needle makes emptying the contents of spoiled eggs easy. A water pik, too, is a handy tool for emptying and washing out these eggs. Whatever method is used, there must be an opening at each end of the egg to prevent a vacuum from building up inside the shell.

Wash the empty egg thoroughly inside and out with cold water, and use a drying rack to drain the clean shells. To remove blemishes, the shell may be scrubbed lightly with an abrasive cleaner or soaked until clean in a mild solution of bleach. Since any hard scrubbing will damage the natural finish, soak the shell in white vinegar before scrubbing to help remove spots. If the shell is to remain white, it should be given a coat of spray fixative to protect against soiling.

If an odor remains in the egg, soak it briefly in a mild solution of bleach and rinse well. Then dry it for several days in a well-ventilated room. If the odor remains, seal the egg by closing both ends with a drop of glue. As a last resort, with a valuable egg which has a large amount of dried yolk inside, place the shell in an open container near an anthill. The ants will clean all animal matter from the shell in a few days.

CUTTING EGGS

The easiest time to cut shells for jewel box or window eggs is when you remove the contents of the egg. A shell becomes brittle after it has been emptied and allowed to dry. Wash the egg well and pencil the cutting line onto the shell.

The egg can be cut with small sturdy scissors or a razor blade. With the point of the scissors, make a small hole in the center of the area to be cut. Cut around the hole, gradually enlarging it and removing only a small amount of shell at a time. Turn the egg so that the scissors are always on the far side of the opening. Gradual cutting reduces chipping and cracking. Another way to reduce chipping is to reinforce the area around the cutting line with transparent tape. Remove the tape after the cutting is finished. Do not try to cut an egg with scissors after the shell has dried.

Because a certain amount of cracking is inevitable, many hobbyists do not use scissors. For hand-cutting, a single-edged razor blade or a utility knife (the kind used for cutting tile and linoleum) gives a much smoother edge and takes only a little more time. A heavy shell such as a goose eggshell can be cut with a razor blade after the shell has dried, but more delicate eggs should be cut while the membranes are still moist. If an egg has dried out, give it a coat of hardening finish or white glue before it is cut. Elaborate cuts or fragile shells should be reinforced with transparent tape before cutting.

With the razor blade, scratch a groove lightly around the pencilled cutting line. Do not try to cut all the way through the shell at once. Before breaking through at any point, go back and forth over the full length of the cutting line until you have cut almost through the shell. This will prevent cut portions of the shell from shifting and cracking. Remove the transparent tape when cutting is completed.

The serious hobbyist may graduate to a power tool for cutting his eggs. A small, lightweight Dremel Moto tool is excellent. A hand-held electric drill of the home workshop variety can be adapted for cutting eggshells by mounting a small grinding wheel in the chuck and cutting with the corner of the wheel. Clamp the drill securely in a vise and hold the egg, turning the cutting line into the grinding wheel. If the egg has spoiled, carefully cut through the shell but not through the membrane. The membrane is surprisingly tough and elastic and can be cut with a razor blade after the grinding is finished. This will keep the yolk from leaking.

The membrane must be removed to provide a smooth surface for paint. It comes out most easily right after the shell has been emptied. Use a toothbrush to scour out a dried membrane. When the interior is not to be painted, leave at least one layer of membrane if it remains firmly in place after the shell is dry, for this strengthens the shell and gives a beautiful sheen to the interior of the egg.

HARDENING EGGS

Small, fragile eggs must be hardened or reinforced, or they will shatter when handled. Larger eggs have a thicker, sturdier shell, and do not have to be hardened unless they are cut extensively, or are to be used and handled frequently.

Coats of white glue, lacquer, fabric, and paint applied as part of the finish will help to strengthen the shell. It can also be hardened significantly by soaking it in or painting it with one part Duco cement thinned with one part acetone or untinted fingernail-polish remover. Wipe off any film of glue that is not absorbed. Hardening should be done after the shell is cut, unless large portions of the shell are to be removed. A hardened shell is much more difficult to cut by hand. Because the solvent in the hardening mixture causes some paints to run, the shell should be hardened before it is painted. An alternative is to apply the hardener to the inside of the shell. Use a medicine dropper to pour diluted cement or white glue inside the egg. Rotate the egg to cover evenly and drain off the excess.

Shells are strengthened somewhat by soaking them in a solution of salt (one tablespoon), soda (one tablespoon), and two quarts of water. Soak the eggs for about one hour, rinse, and drain them on a drying rack. An egg can be made very sturdy by gluing several layers of paper toweling into it as a lining. Liquid solder may be used to strengthen arches or windows cut out of an egg. It is applied from the tube in a thin layer spread over the entire area. Transparent tape can be used in concealed areas to permanently reinforce the shell.

Broken and cracked shells can be repaired and decorated with considerable success, although this is usually done only on larger and scarcer varieties of eggs. Conceal repairs inside the egg under a lining or within the design, then harden the egg with white glue or diluted Duco cement to prevent further breakage. Cracks are repaired with transparent tape applied in small pieces to conform to the curve of the shell. Glue and liquid solder can also be spread over a slightly cracked or crushed area.

When applied according to package directions, gesso can be used to reinforce eggshells and to repair broken ones. Gesso changes the texture of the shell, so try it on a piece of broken shell beforehand. The slightly rough, textured surface which gesso creates is very effective with some paints and finishes. Save shells that are completely broken for experimenting with new finishes and techniques.

PROTECTIVE FINISHES

Unless they are protected, the paints and fabrics used on eggs will soil and the metallic trims will tarnish. The easiest way to protect an entire egg is to spray it with a clear coat of fixative. Before putting on the final coats of fixative, however, remove all traces of white glue with a cotton swab moistened with water, and erase all pencil marks. Clean off any fingerprints and trim loose ends of braid and fabric.

There are a variety of fixatives available that provide either a dull matte or a shiny gloss finish; the choice is determined by the style of the egg. Select the finishes in aerosol form. Clear plastic sprays and gloss lacquers give excellent high-gloss results. Artists' fixatives, used to set pastel drawings and watercolors, will give your eggs a protective matte finish; your art supply dealer can help you select these products. If neither is available, you can make your own by diluting clear shellac with wood alcohol and applying it with a small spray gun. Or you can spray or paint clear varnish on the egg. Even clear fingernail polish can be used, if it is thinned slightly with untinted fingernail polish remover or acetone; apply it with a brush.

All finishes should be applied in several thin coats to prevent dripping. Spray finishes, for example, tend to pool when applied heavily. Some fixatives cause certain paints to bleed, so test both paint and fixative on a piece of broken shell before spraying a finished egg. If the eggs are lined up on a drying rack, several can be sprayed at one time. Again, spray lightly and let each coat dry thoroughly before applying the next. Also be sure that you don't touch any egg whose finish is still damp, or you'll mar it with fingerprints.

All protective finishes should be put on before the jewels, nonmetallic sequins, and velvet, since they tend to dull the jewels and matte the fabric. Brush up the pile with a clean toothbrush if any lacquer or glue does get on it.

All metallic braids, gold and silver papers, metallic sequins, and metallic paints must be protected from tarnishing. Avoid getting fingerprints on them before they have been given a protective coating. A coat of clear finish may be brushed on metallic braids and papers before they are applied to the egg or sprayed on afterwards. Brushing gives better coverage to braids, but can cause them to run. Clear fingernail polish is excellent to brush on braids. A drop or two on the end of the braid will prevent raveling.

Dyes and paints should be protected against soil and rubbing. Dye, chalk, and antiquing glazes mar easily and should be given a coat of fixative before the egg is further decorated. Glued-on pictures, découpage, dried butterflies, and flowers all need many coats of protective finish to prevent chipping and tearing.

Fabrics used on eggs can be sprayed with a soil-repellent aerosol product sold for use on clothing.

HANGING AND STORING EGGS

Eggs to be hung on a Christmas tree, an Easter egg tree, or a mobile must have a loop of some sort attached at the top. Slip a wire Christmas ornament hanger through this loop to hang the eggs (Figure 1 and Plate 1).

Sometimes a hanger can be part of the overall design of the egg. A strip of velvet or grosgrain ribbon, a lightweight chain or metallic braid glued around the egg lengthwise provides a loop at the top. Allow the glue to dry overnight before hanging the egg.

When an invisible hanger is needed, use nylon mono-filament fishline; it is strong and easy to handle. With a long needle, thread a double strand of line through the center of the egg from end to end. Bring the needle back through the holes, leaving a loop at the top of the egg, and tie a hard knot at the bottom. Secure the line to the shell at both ends with a drop of white glue. Let the glue dry overnight before the egg is hung.

FIGURE 1 Window eggs hung with Christmas ornament hangers.

By Mrs. F. R. Lawson

Eggs for mobiles may need to be weighted for balance. With a funnel, pour a small amount of sand inside one end. When the mobile is balanced and the nylon line attached, close both ends of the egg with a drop of white glue. Eggs used as Christmas tree ornaments will often hang more gracefully if they are lightly weighted.

To store hens' eggs, put them in egg cartons and label each box. Shipping boxes for wine bottles often have dividers which are perfect for storing larger eggs. The dividers can be cut down to the height of the eggs. Soft-drink bottle cartons that have six or eight sections will hold goose eggs nicely.

PEDESTALS

Many eggs are mounted on stands or pedestals (Figure 2), the size of which depends on the size of the egg. Household items found in dime and hardware stores can be covered or painted for use as pedestals. Gold and pearlized collars designed for this purpose are sold by mail-order houses. Try stacking several to create a tall, elegant stand. You will think of many more if you look at familiar household items. Here are just a few of the items which can be used as pedestals:

Drawer pulls Wooden drawer pulls, 1 or 1¼ inch, can be made into pedestals by sanding the tops so that they stand flat and gluing them upside down on the egg. China or brass drawer pulls are made to stand flat by gluing a small round piece of cardboard to the top.

Knobs Half-inch or smaller brass drawer-knobs make unusual pedestals (Plate 6).

Lids Try using glass percolator tops, small cosmetic containers and their lids, or lids from liquid soap dispensers and toothpaste tubes.

Spools Cut a wooden thread spool in half for use as a pedestal.

Rings Glue a stack of wooden curtain rings together or try wedding bands, particularly the wide, ornate ones.

Other Eggs A small piece of eggshell cut from the end of the egg, or a small whole egg standing on end can serve as a pedestal. Reinforce any eggshell that is used for a stand.

Candleholders Parts of lamp bases or brass candlesticks can often be unscrewed. Use a section as a base for an egg. Remove the spike from a small blossom-shaped candleholder with wire cutters.

FIGURE 2 Box eggs mounted on jewelled stands and trimmed with metallic enamels and "found" materials.

You can also make pedestals from pieces of styrofoam, balsa wood, or cardboard. All these pedestals can be painted to match the egg, sprayed with metallic paint, antiqued, or covered with fabric and Mystik tape.

An egg can rest on three or four small feet instead of a pedestal (Plate 4). Tiny brass pulls, marbles, and large pearls make very nice feet. To glue on pearl feet, position the pearls on a terry-cloth towel. With a toothpick, put a drop of glue on top of each pearl and set the egg down on the pearls. The terry cloth will keep the pearls from rolling until the glue dries. Pearls can be stacked to make legs (Plate 18) or mounted in a ring around the base of the egg. Handle marble feet in the same manner.

2
PAINTED EGGS
AND SPECIAL EFFECTS

PAINTED AND COLORED EGGS

Many kinds of paint can be used on eggs: acrylics, tempera, poster paint, or enamel. Food colors can also be used. Each imparts its own style to the egg.

Before they are painted, eggs should be clean and dry. If the egg is to be hardened, do this before painting it. The design can be lightly sketched on the egg with a hard pencil because acrylic paints and enamels are opaque enough to hide the pencil lines. Do not use pencil with food colors or very pale acrylic colors, however; the lines will show through. Erase any pencil errors with a moist cotton swab.

Background scenes which tell a story or represent a nursery rhyme can be painted on the inside of window and box eggs. It is essential, however, to remove all traces of membrane before beginning to paint, since membrane can chip and peel. The same techniques are used for painting both the inside and outside of the egg. Remember that all painting should be protected with a coat of clear finish.

Acrylics

Acrylic paint is very versatile. It is recommended for painting scenes and designs on eggshells as well as for overall coloring. Because it is water soluble, acrylic paint is easy to use. A set of small tubes in a variety of colors is well worth the

Spring scene drawn on a white egg.

Spring scene drawn on a white egg.

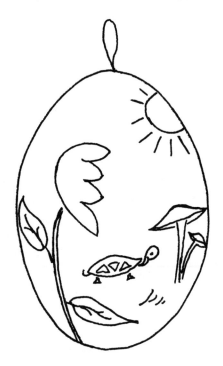

investment, although only the basic colors are essential because acrylics can be mixed easily.

This type of paint can be applied straight from the tube or thinned with water. When applied from the tube, acrylics are handled much like oil paint and give a similar effect. Squeeze a small amount of each color onto a palette or china plate and mix as desired. To thin the paint, squeeze a small amount of color into a muffin tin and add water a drop at a time until the desired consistency is obtained. Diluted with water, the paint resembles watercolors or tempera. When small amounts are used, as in a design on an egg, water-reduced acrylics can be handled on a china plate or a large plastic lid.

If it has not completely dried, acrylic paint can be washed off the shell. When dry, it can be painted over, for it does not chip or peel. Whether the finish is matte or glossy is determined by the fixative used. Brushes used with acrylic can be cleaned with water. Use several small ones for fine painting and larger ones for painting entire eggs.

Ideas for Painting with Acrylics

1. For a quick collection of Christmas tree ornaments, paint hardened hens' eggs in deep shades of rose, turquoise, fuchsia, blue, and emerald. Two or three coats of paint are necessary for even coverage. Spray the eggs with a matte or gloss finish. Circle each egg with a loop of velvet ribbon mounted on a strip of gold paper. Select velvet in shades that are lighter than the colors used on the eggs. For variation, use pastel shades of paint and encircle the eggs with darker shades of same colors.

2. Paint white or pastel hens' eggs with seasonal motifs copied from the profusion of cards and other material available.

3. At Easter, paint little spring scenes around white eggs. These can be as simple or as detailed as your taste and talents dictate. Try flowers, mushrooms, trees, rabbits, chipmunks, frogs, and birds. Paint twining vines, sprays of flowers, pastoral scenes, etc., on eggs (Plate 2). Give the egg a porcelainlike finish with glue (see page 19). Ring the finished egg with gold paper.

4. Paint three to five big, bold red and orange daisies on each white egg or paint big yellow daisies and red ladybugs (Figure 3).

5. Paint faces on eggs. Have one resemble Humpty Dumpty, as in Figure 3. Make one egg for each member of the family and hide them at Easter.

FIGURE 3   Hens' eggs painted with flowers, animals, and faces.

6. Paint the egg to resemble an animal such as a mouse, an owl, or an imaginary animal. For a mouse, use the pointed end of the egg for the head; paint on the eyes and mouth; and cut feet, ears, and tail from paper and glue them on. To make a stork, use an egg for the body and pipe cleaners for the legs. Make small holes in the egg, insert the pipe cleaners and secure them with a drop of glue. Make several storks as party favors for a baby shower. Paint an egg to resemble a peacock, using a pipe-cleaner neck and a feather tail.

7. For the Fourth of July paint stars and sunbursts in red and blue on white eggs.

8. Copy Pennsylvania Dutch folk designs and American Indian designs onto eggs.

9. Paint geometric designs onto eggs. Use a tape measure to make accurate lines.

10. If you are adept with a brush, try copying Japanese watercolor paintings onto eggshells. With a small shader brush you can paint flowers like those on hand-painted china.

Paint eggs to resemble animals, using paper ears, legs, and tails.

PAINTED EGGS AND SPECIAL EFFECTS

Enamel and Metallic Spray Paints

Both spray and brush-on enamels are marvelous on eggs, as are gold, silver, and copper metallic spray paints. Use leftover cans of automotive touch-up paint to give eggs a beautiful metallic finish.

To use spray paints, turn a large cardboard box on its side. Hold the egg and the spray can inside the box to paint, keeping the can at least 12 inches from the eggs. The box will catch the excess paint.

Several thin coats of aerosol paint are more satisfactory than one heavy coat. Take care to avoid drips. Follow the directions on the can and be sure to keep the nozzle clean to avoid having to throw away half-filled cans because of paint-clogged nozzles. All metallic paints should be given a final coat of clear protective finish to prevent tarnishing.

A window or box egg can be sprayed one color on the outside and another on the inside. Spray the inside first, and after it dries, thoroughly mask it with paper toweling; then spray the outside. Try silver on the inside and gold on the outside, or deep rose inside and pale pink outside.

The tiny jars of paint used for model cars and airplanes are excellent for eggs. These come in almost every color and are very useful for painting designs on eggs that have an overall coat of metallic spray paint.

One manufacturer of these paints sells several beautifully vivid colors of metal-flake paints. They tend to streak but they are worth the effort needed to produce a smooth coat. First, paint the egg with enamel or acrylics of the same color as the metal-flake paint. Let this base coat dry thoroughly. Then apply the enamel with a wide brush, using long, broad strokes. Do not go back over your work. Shake the jar well before starting and stir frequently to keep it from settling.

When the first coat of metal-flake paint is not quite dry, apply a second coat with the same quick, broad strokes. Again, do not try to smooth it out or go back over it. If necessary, apply a third coat. Allow it to dry overnight. (Do not try this method in humid weather; the paint won't dry.) Any minor irregularities in the finish will be inconspicuous when the egg is trimmed. This finish is most beautiful when the egg is jewelled or trimmed with gold papers and velvet ribbon. See red and blue box eggs in Plate 16.

Ideas for Painting with Enamels and Metallic Spray Paints

1. The brilliant hues of enamels and metallic spray-paints make memorable Christmas tree ornaments. Spray-painting eggs is so easy that you can make enough to

completely decorate a small tree. Line the eggs up on a drying rack and spray-paint them all at one time with gold and silver; then spray them with fixative. Hang each egg with a loop of velvet ribbon in a different bright color. Try red velvet on gold eggs, and blue velvet on silver eggs.

2. Paint a holiday design on each egg with model-paint enamels. Make geometric patterns by slipping a wide rubber band around the egg from end to end and painting a line on each side of it. Remove the band, and paint a row of diamonds, triangles, or scrolls inside the lines (Plate 3).

3. Paint eggs in red, green, yellow, and blue enamel, and trim them with loops of velvet in contrasting colors or with loops of metallic braid (Plate 3). The yellow egg in Plate 2 is enamelled and decorated with gold cord. Do not overlap the cord. Instead, cut it at junctions.

4. Glue sequins in rows around enamelled eggshells. Use a color lighter than the enamel or one that contrasts sharply with it.

5. Trim enamelled eggs with glitter glued on in bold designs. (Plate 3).

6. With model paint, draw a Christmas tree on each side of a white egg. Trim the tree with sequins (Plate 3).

7. Paint a Santa, angels, or stars on eggs with model enamels or cut pictures from wrapping paper and greeting cards to glue on enamelled eggs. Hang the eggs with a loop of velvet ribbon (Plate 3).

Dye

You may want to try tinting eggs with Easter egg or fabric dye. Mix the dye according to the directions on the package. Many dyes can be kept for several days in tightly closed containers, although those containing vinegar will corrode metal jar lids.

Though it is not necessary to remove the contents before dyeing, eggs will dye more evenly if this is done. Boiling eggs removes oils from the shell and causes uneven coloring. Dry, empty shells often color unevenly, too. The shell should be clean and dry. Check it for blemishes or hairline cracks. If the egg is not empty, the dye must be cool; hot dye will partially cook the egg. Completely immerse the egg or gently rotate it to ensure even coverage. The longer the egg is left in the dye, the deeper the color will be. A damp egg can be dipped in one color and then in another to produce a third color. For example, alternately dipping in red and yellow dye will produce an orange egg. Dry the egg on a cake rack and give it a coat of spray fixative.

Dyeing is a very efficient way to color a large number of eggs quickly. Darker colors, however, are difficult to obtain and they are not very stable. Goose eggs do not always absorb dyes evenly, and usually better results are obtained by painting the empty shell with acrylic paints.

Pastel Chalks

Pastel chalks retain the natural texture and patina of the eggshell and give it a velvety finish. Do not use wax or oil chalks, which resist spraying with a fixative.

The shell may first be sprayed with a coat of lacquer, but this is not absolutely necessary. Rub the selected colored chalk on a piece of fine sandpaper. Transfer the dust from the sandpaper to the egg with your finger. Blow or brush off the excess chalk with a soft tissue and spray the egg with a matte fixative. To obtain a deeper shade, alternate several coats of chalk with several coats of fixative, ending with the fixative. Handle the egg as little as possible before the fixative is applied to prevent disturbing the chalk.

Ideas for Using Pastel Chalks

1. Trim the finished egg with pastel velvet or grosgrain ribbon, or gold paper.
2. Pastels combine very well with jewelling to make unique Christmas tree ornaments. Pastels can also be used to color the inside of box eggs or to blend in découpage. See the large egg in Figure 10 and the pink egg in Plate 8.
3. Designs and pictures can be drawn on the egg with chalk. Blend and soften the chalk lines by rubbing them with your finger.

SPECIAL EFFECTS

Ivory

Some brands of plastic sprays will give an ivory color and finish to eggshells. The egg can be painted ivory and then given several coats of clear plastic spray finish.

Watercolor

Watercolors do not react successfully on shells because they bead on the nonporous surface. However, a watercolor effect can be achieved with either acrylic paints diluted in water or full-strength food coloring. Acrylic paint is easier to handle but if it is not available, try the inexpensive food colors.

Food coloring is used as it comes from the container, and the colors can be mixed or diluted with water to form a wash.

Use very small brushes and a technique similar to watercolor painting for lovely pastoral scenes, sprays of flowers, and tiny portraits.

When these eggs are given a porcelainlike finish, as described on page 19, they resemble pieces of fine, hand-painted china. These miniature paintings may be framed with gold découpage papers glued to the eggshell before the final coats of finish are sprayed on. Or spray the finished painting with a matte fixative and circle the egg with a loop of velvet ribbon in a harmonizing color.

Marbleizing

Eggs can be given a marbleized or pearlized finish with fingernail polish used alone or in combination with waterproof felt-tipped marking pens.

Paint an egg with several coats of pearlized or pastel nail polish; trim with lace and pastel jewels. The irregularities of a nail-polish finish add to the marbleized appearance (Plate 17).

For a darker, more heavily marbled finish, draw areas and splotches of color, and lines of veining, under the nail polish with felt-tipped pens. The solvent in the polish causes the ink to run, blending the varicolored areas to give the marbleized effect. Experiment on broken shells until you get exactly the effect you want.

Select marking pens in several colors. Working on one section at a time, color the egg with the pens in stripes or random patches of color. Immediately go over these areas with pearlized or pastel nail polish before the ink has a chance to dry. The direction of your brush strokes will vary the design. Repeat this procedure, section by section, until the egg is completely coated. You can apply several layers of finish by alternating ink and nail polish, ending with nail polish.

Experiment with enamels and acrylic paints. Both will run if coated with nail polish or orange shellac before they are dry.

Ideas for Marbleized Eggs

1. Using red, yellow, and black felt-tipped pens, make color patches all over the egg and go over it with pink nail polish.
2. Use a black felt-tipped marker to draw veins on an egg painted gold. Go over it with orange nail polish.
3. Color the egg with red and yellow felt-tipped markers. Go over it with pink nail polish. Draw black veins on the polish and go over the egg with another coat of pink nail polish (Plate 2).
4. Select a model paint that does not completely cover the egg with the first coat. Apply it in swirling designs with a

wide brush. The blue-green egg in Plate 3 was done this way.

5. Coat an egg with pink, pearlized nail polish. When the polish becomes "tacky," use a soft brush to pick up torn pieces of gold leaf and touch them down on the nail polish. Do not try to cover the egg completely with the leaf. Cracks and tears add to the marble effect. Give the whole egg another coat of nail polish or spray lacquer. The pink and gold egg in Plate 2 has this finish.

6. Use nail polish alone to paint the outside of a window egg (Figure 40).

7. Line a box egg with one of these marble finishes.

Enamel on Gold

A spectacular finish, suggestive of enamel on gold, can be created with waterproof felt-tipped marking pens and pastel nail polish. Spray the egg with gold paint and allow it to dry completely. With a felt-tipped pen (red is very effective), color one section of the egg at a time. The direction of the strokes will show on the finished egg so they should all go in the same direction. Apply the color lightly so that the gold shows through. Before the ink has dried, go over it with pastel nail polish, always brushing in the same direction. Color the entire egg this way. Apply a second coat of very light pastel or clear nail polish to the entire egg. This finish makes a marvelous background for gold papers and jewels. Many aerosol model paints have a translucent quality and with practice you can spray them over gold so that the gold shows through.

Miscellaneous Finishes

Use felt-tipped pens or India ink to draw faces and work designs on eggs. Try a psychedelic or modern overall design. Finish by gluing on a few sequins in a contrasting color to accent the design (Plate 2).

American Indian designs and other folk art motifs can be drawn on the egg with felt-tipped marking pens. They are then "aged" by applying an antiquing glaze or orange shellac. Finish with a coat of matte fixative.

Many other mediums can be used on the versatile egg. Experiment with them or try combinations of those suggested. For example, draw outline designs with India ink on top of acrylic paint. Whichever type of paint is used, the entire egg should be protected with at least one coat of spray fixative.

Watch for new products such as spray leather, liquid metals, etc. Many of these can be effectively used on eggs.

Ballantine

Ballantine is a craft material available from Taylor House that gives a textured, sparkling appearance to a surface. It is particularly effective when combined with cutouts. The ballantine consists of very small translucent balls that reflect light. To make the ballantined egg in Plate 4, cut a goose egg in half, and paint it with metallic copper enamel. Glue on flowers cut from gift-wrap paper. Coat the entire shell with white glue and pour the ballantine over it until the egg is coated. Catch the excess ballantine in a box and reuse it. Allow yourself plenty of working space as ballantine tends to scatter. Let the egg dry undisturbed. The beauty and texture of this finish is not apparent until it is dry. Finish the edge with gold braid.

The window egg in Plate 5 was painted pale green and lined with ballantine to complement the glass swan. The Siamese cat egg in Figure 34 was also lined with ballantine which contributes to the rich appearance of this egg. See page 69 for directions on completing the swan egg, and page 67 for the cat egg.

Porcelain Finish

There are several ways to achieve a porcelainlike finish on an eggshell. They are all based on the principle that many thin coats of a transparent material applied over paint give the appearance of a deep glaze. Eggs that are painted, dyed, or decorated with cutout pictures are beautiful under a porcelainlike finish. Pastel colors are very elegant, too. Unblemished eggs can be left white.

The black egg in Plate 6 has cutout pictures découpaged *under* layers of glue and lacquer. The vase-shaped egg in Plate 5 has flowers painted with acrylics under the glue. The pink and green eggs in Plate 4 and all the eggs in Figures 13, 15, and 16 have been given a porcelain finish.

The quickest way to produce such a finish is to apply five or six coats of glossy spray lacquer after the shell has been painted. Instead of spray lacquer, you can use the brush-on kind, if you wish; or use clear, high-gloss varnish. Each of these will give a hard, durable finish and an appearance of depth.

A more time-consuming method involves applying numerous coats of Elmer's white glue, followed by four to six coats of high-gloss lacquer. Paint the egg first and glue on any découpage cutouts. All pictures are glued in place and all painting is done before the glue coats are applied. When all paint and glue is completely dry, apply six to ten coats of full-strength Elmer's white glue, letting each coat dry thoroughly before applying the next. A drying rack is almost essential when working with wet, glue-covered eggs. Save time by doing several eggs at once. In dry weather approximately three coats of glue may be applied each day. The glue should become completely transparent between each coat.

The glue should be applied with a ½-inch or larger brush and must go on the egg evenly. It must not be allowed to bead, streak, or drip. If drips and streaks do develop, the egg can be soaked in water and the glue carefully washed off. Sometimes a waxiness on the shell interferes with the adherence of the glue; in this case, scrubbing helps. Wash the shell thoroughly in soap and water, scrub lightly with scouring powder, rinse it in vinegar and then in clear water, repaint it, and start over. Hand lotions can come off on the shell and interfere with the glue also.

When spreading glue, be sure that your fingers are absolutely dry and free of glue. If they stick to the egg, they will leave a print or even pull up several layers of finish.

When applying glue over a painted or glued-on picture, take care not to smear the design. Full-strength glue will not usually affect acrylic paint that has dried overnight; however, an occasional pigment will separate into its primary colors. Such colors can be sealed with a coat of spray fixative. Some cheaply printed magazine pictures smear very easily. Test them before gluing them to the egg. They can be sealed with an aerosol fixative. Avoid working the glue excessively; lay it evenly over the design with a minimum of brushwork. If any cloudiness appears, no further coats of glue should be added. Cloudiness will usually disappear if the egg is dried for several days before the lacquer is put on. Cloudiness often occurs in damp weather and will clear up when the weather changes.

Some hobbyists recommend diluting Elmer's glue with water until it spreads easily, and applying as many as twenty-five coats. The individual's preferences and time limitations will dictate the technique he chooses.

Follow the glue with at least four coats of high-gloss spray lacquer. Put on at least two coats before handling the egg. Put on two more coats after the metallic trims and the gold découpage papers have been glued in place.

Ideas for a Porcelainlike Finish

1. Tiny flowers can be modelled in the fine white clay sold for making ceramic jewelry and glued to an egg. Roll tiny balls of clay and flatten them against the palm of the hand

with the finger. Shape them so that they curve slightly. Each one becomes a single leaf or petal. When they are dry, spray them with fixative and paint them with acrylic or ceramic paint. Glue them to each other and to the egg. Flowers and eggshell together are given about five coats of Elmer's glue followed by four coats of gloss lacquer. Figure 4 shows a goose egg painted lavender (lavender bleeds and must be sealed before applying glue). It is trimmed with clay violets and finished with gold découpage paper.

Ukrainian Pysanky

Pysanky is a highly developed folk art that uses wax and natural dyes to create elaborate designs on whole, raw eggs (Plate 7). The simplified version of this intricate technique is easy to master.

The basic design is drawn on the egg with melted wax. The colors are added in successive layers, beginning with the lightest and ending with the darkest. As the dyeing progresses, additional portions of the design are drawn with hot wax. Successive dyeings will not color the waxed portions of the egg, so that each section remains the color it was when it was waxed. The wax is all removed after the final dyeing.

Hens' eggs are more amenable to this technique than goose eggs. The uneven texture of the goose egg tends to hold the wax and sometimes takes the dyes unevenly. However, with patience, lovely effects can be produced on the larger eggs. Cool Easter-egg dye, fabric dye, or dye especially formulated for pysanky can be used. Follow the directions on the package for preparing the dye.

Select white, blemish-free eggs. Hold the egg up to the light and examine it for hairline cracks that will mar the design. The Ukrainians use whole raw eggs because they absorb dyes more evenly and give a finer result. After several months the contents dry up inside the shell. Commercial eggs, however, sometimes rot and explode instead of drying up. For any but the serious student of pysanky, freshly blown, empty eggs are the most practical.

It is possible to remove the contents of a raw egg after dyeing is finished. The dye must be completely sealed with shellac or fixative and care must be taken to avoid any moisture or egg white touching the dyed surface.

All eggs should be handled with a clean paper towel. Oil and

FIGURE 4   Lavender goose egg trimmed with clay violets and finished with gold découpage paper.

lotions from the hands will affect the dyes and leave blemishes on the finished egg.

The design should be planned in advance on a piece of paper. Successive colors will combine. For example, dyeing first in yellow and then in blue will produce green on unwaxed portions of the egg. This must be considered in planning the design.

Pencil lines on the egg will show through Easter-egg dyes and light colors. When it is necessary to pencil in a design, use light lines drawn with a hard lead. When drawing a geometric design, slip a wide rubber band over the egg from end to end or around its center to provide guidelines. Draw along the rubber band with the wax and then slip the band off the egg.

Light an ordinary household candle, letting it burn until a pool of melted wax forms at the base of the wick. Heat a fine or medium-fine Speedball pen tip in the flame, and dip it into the melted wax. Using the melted wax like ink, draw over those portions of the design that are to remain white. The pen point will need to be refilled frequently by first heating it in the flame and then dipping it in the melted wax. Care must be taken not to blot the wax. With a little practice you will perfect this technique. It is very difficult to erase errors on the egg, but they can sometimes be incorporated into the design.

Beeswax is easier to use than candlewax. Simply melt the beeswax over water in a small pan. Heat the pen point or kistka (a wax applicator) in a candle flame and dip it into the melted beeswax.

When all of the design that is to remain white is covered with wax, the egg is dipped in the lightest color dye (usually yellow). Be very careful not to chip or disturb the wax while dyeing the egg. When the egg has reached the desired shade of yellow, carefully remove it from the dye and let it dry. With hot wax, draw all portions of the design that are to remain yellow and dye the egg the next shade (for example, orange). Let the egg dry and wax in all portions that are to remain orange. To cover large areas with wax, use a small brush, working quickly before the brush stiffens. The brush can be cleaned in hot water. Continue waxing and dyeing the egg in successively darker colors until the design is complete. Handle the egg carefully; it is easy to scratch the dye which has built up on the shell.

Place the egg on a paper towel in a small pan in a warm (150° F) oven. (This temperature will not cook raw eggs.) When

Mrs. F. R. Lawson

PLATE 1 Dried plant material and soft colors complement the figures in these window eggs.

PLATE 3 Hens' eggs make charming Christmas tree ornaments.

PLATE 2 Colorful, easy-to-make hens' eggs decorated with a variety of household materials.

the wax becomes shiny, remove the egg and wipe off the wax with absorbent towelling. It may be necessary to put the egg in the oven several times to remove all the wax. Spray the finished egg immediately with fixative or coat it with clear shellac.

The Ukrainians traditionally use stylized birds, flowers, and geometric patterns, but this technique is equally handsome when done in other styles. Consider Mexican, German, and American folk art for inspiration. Pure geometric patterns are perhaps easiest for the beginner and are very striking.

A similar method uses only one dyeing. The entire design is waxed onto the white or pastel egg, and the egg is then dyed to a deep shade. Line drawings, pen-and-ink sketches, and scrollwork designs lend themselves very well to this approach. For example, the elaborate Chinese dragon in Plate 7 was drawn on a white hen's egg with a fine-tipped fountain pen. The egg was then dyed a deep Chinese red produced by alternately dipping the egg in red and orange dye until a dark shade was reached.

The Central Europeans also decorate eggs by dyeing them a dark shade and then scratching a design in the dye with the point of a knife or a needle. The rooster on the purple egg in Plate 7 was done this way. The result is similar to the single-dye technique described above.

The Appendix of this book lists a mail-order source of supplies for Ukrainian eggs. Pictures of finished eggs, special dyes, beeswax, kistkas, and directions for making the eggs are also available. The serious craftsman will be interested in special dyes for pysanky, fabric, and batik which are available in more colors and in deeper shades than ordinary dyes.

Plate 7 shows a variety of methods for making Ukrainian eggs. The two orange eggs and the blue and purple egg were made with candlewax, Easter-egg dyes, and an ordinary pen. The geometric designs were made with a kistka, beeswax, and pysanky dyes.

Leaded Eggs

With this technique a lattice is created by applying liquid solder in delicate lines, thus supporting the shell sufficiently to permit cutting away large portions of it.

Empty and clean the shell, and pencil in a filigree design. Go over the pencil lines with Lepage's liquid solder. Apply it from the tube with a light, steady pressure, working in long, even strokes. The solder will shrink as it dries. Go back over it until enough coats have been applied to make a thick, raised design.

FIGURE 5   Large portion of eggshell can be cut away, creating a filigree design.

With small scissors carefully snip away the exposed shell leaving only the soldered lines. Or leave portions of the exposed shell intact for use as part of the design. They may be dyed before the shell is cut as the dye will not tint the solder. Dyeing after the shell is cut will color the inside of the egg. The solder can be sprayed silver, painted, or left its natural lead color.

Ideas for Leaded Eggs

1. To make the hen's egg shown in Figure 5, draw a series of spiralling lines from the top to the bottom of the egg. Link the lines with a ring of circles around the equator of the egg. Go over the lines with liquid solder and cut away the exposed shell. Glue sequins in the circular center section.
2. Draw lines from the top to the bottom of the egg so that they cross the concentric rings around the egg. Cut away the rectangles between the lines.
3. Draw a diamond pattern or rows of circles on an egg. Cut away the inside of each circle or diamond.
4. Mount tiny figurines or candles inside lattice eggs. Use small birthday candles and secure them with a drop of hot

PLATE 4 Goose eggs made into miniature jewel boxes.

PLATE 5 Many different cuts are possible on large eggs.

PLATE 6 Two goose eggs in the style of Russian Easter eggs.

PLATE 7 Pysanky eggs.

PLATE 9 Gold-leafed carriage egg, open.
Mary Sammartino

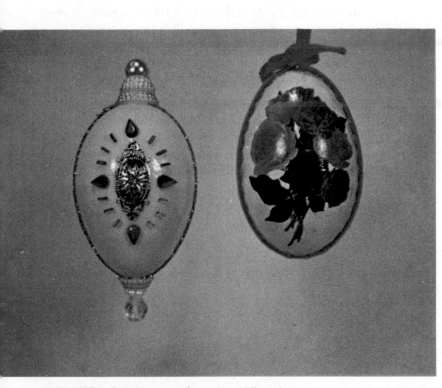

PLATE 8 Pendant eggs: formal and Victorian.

wax in the bottom of the egg. Stand each egg on a small metal drawer pull, or on a branch of a modern candelabrum. Secure the eggs in the candelabrum with hot wax.

5. Spray-paint parts of the egg with gold paint before the shell is cut away.

6. Dye the inside of the egg after the shell is removed.

7. Mount a collection of lattice eggs on a string of miniature Christmas tree lights. Before mounting them, make sure all the bulbs on the string are working. Draw a circle of lead at the top of each egg large enough for the bulb to slip through when the shell inside the circle is cut away. After the shells are cut away, complete the eggs in various designs and paint them if desired. Insert the light bulb in the circular hole at the top of each shell and seal it in place with epoxy glue. Follow directions on the epoxy container. A string of these lights will cast fascinating shadows.

8. Use a lead lattice for the window of a window egg.

9. To make the lattice box in Figure 5 and Plate 16, cut a goose egg in half. Draw a lattice on the top half of the shell, leaving a ¼ inch wide strip intact around the edge. Outline the lattice with lead. Coat the rest of the top half of the shell with lead, and let it dry. Glue a jar lid to the bottom half to make a pedestal. Coat the bottom half with lead, applying it unevenly and in a thick coat to give an interesting texture. When both halves of the shell are dry, antique it by coating it with brown cream shoe polish. Wipe off the excess. Let the polish dry and spray it with matte fixative. Using small sturdy pointed scissors, carefully snip away the portions of shell between the lattice.

Line the shell in two steps. First glue red satin or a similar fabric on the inside, over the open portions of the lattice. Very lightly, wipe excess glue off the fabric with a cotton swab moistened with water. When the glue has dried thoroughly, both halves of the shell are completely lined with the same fabric. Put a second layer of fabric right over the first on the top half of the shell. Follow the directions given on page 50 for lining the egg.

Trim the outside of the egg as desired with metallic braids. On one egg done in this fashion, an antique silver chain from a piece of costume jewelry was hung in loops around the bottom.

3
COVERED
AND JEWELLED EGGS

All the techniques discussed in this section are equally beautiful when used to line an egg or cover a jewel box or window egg. Each method has a distinctive style of its own and should be considered when planning the inside of window eggs or additional trims for box eggs.

COVERED EGGS

Eggs can be decorated by covering them with various materials. Pieces of fabric, leather, wallpaper, beads, and cord can completely cover eggs. Cutout pictures, gold papers, butterflies, and dried flowers add character to your eggs. Small eggs should be hardened before they are covered. Fabric coverings can be sprayed with a dirt repellent. White glue is always used, unless otherwise specified. Use toothpicks to spread the glue.

Patchwork

Patchwork designs are created by covering the egg with soft fabrics such as gingham, silk, velvet, or soft leather. Figure 6 shows an egg covered in bits of blue and white gingham. Eggs completely covered in soft leather are handsome when hung with lengths of fine gold or silver chain. You can combine materials such as cork wallpaper, pieces of suede, and smooth leather.

FIGURE 6 Hen's egg covered with pieces of blue and white gingham.

PLATE 10 Angel eggs for the Christmas tree.   Mrs. F. R. Lawson

PLATE 11 A goose egg decorated as
          a tiny Christmas house.

PLATE 12 Triptych egg.

PLATE 13 Whimsical window eggs.

PLATE 15 Custard the Dragon.

PLATE 14 Empire egg.

Mrs. F. R. Lawson

Work out a patchwork pattern on paper. Cut the fabric pieces according to the paper pattern and glue them to the egg with white glue. The individual pieces of material must be small enough to adjust to the curve of the egg without wrinkling. It is much easier to spread the glue on the shell than on the fabric. Begin at the equator of the egg and work toward the ends. The shape of the individual pieces must be altered slightly as the curve of the shell changes.

Ideas for Patchwork Eggs

1. Make a checkerboard with two fabrics. Select two plain fabrics in contrasting colors or two different prints. Cut the fabric into small squares. The squares for each succeeding row must be cut slightly smaller. Start at the equator of the egg and glue the fabric around the egg in rows of alternating colors. Do not spiral around the egg.

2. Cut diamond-shaped pieces to form a star at each end of the egg. Cover the rest of the egg with triangles in alternating colors.

3. Cover an egg with stripes of alternating colors or with stripes running in two directions to suggest a plaid.

4. Use scraps of leather or construction paper instead of fabric.

5. Cover an egg with soft leather from an old glove. Cover the ends with gold paper. Mount a pearl collar and a large pearl on each end. To hang the egg, thread nylon monofilament fishline through the egg, through both finials, and through a length of fine gold chain.

6. Combine pieces of cork wallpaper and suede.

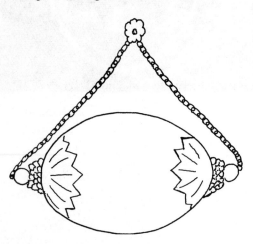

Covered egg hung on nylon monofilament fishline threaded through both finials and a length of fine gold chain.

Lace

Lace makes a delicate covering for an eggshell. First paint the egg a color which will accent or contrast with the lace. Ribbon lace (½ inch or narrower) is the easiest to handle. Working from the center of the egg toward the ends, coat one small section of shell at a time with glue, and smooth on the lace in rows around the shell. Avoid getting glue on top of the lace or on your fingers. When the glue is dry, trim the excess from around the edges and finish the edges with narrow grosgrain or velvet ribbon.

Ideas for Lace-Covered Eggs

1. Figure 14 shows a jewel-box goose egg painted with pink enamel and finished with ½-inch white lace. It is lined

(see chapter on box eggs) with white velvet and trimmed on the outside with ¼-inch rose velvet ribbon, pearls, and rhinestones. The stand is a bottle cap, covered with the same velvet ribbon. Also see Plate 18.

2. Weave grosgrain ribbon through the lace before gluing it in place.
3. Combine lace and metallic braids on an egg.
4. Cut out individual designs from lace yard goods and glue them on a painted egg.

Embroidery Floss

Eggs can also be covered with embroidery floss. Use all six strands of the floss just as it comes from the package. Coat one part of the egg at a time with glue, beginning at the equator. Wind the floss around and around the egg, keeping the strands close together and the rows straight. Begin and end each color on the same side of the egg so that the seam is not conspicuous. Try stripes of varying widths in different colors. Multicolored floss is very pretty when used this way.

Simple designs such as large daisies can be worked out with embroidery floss. Outline the design on the egg in pencil. Starting at the outside edge of the design, wind the thread around within the outline until the flower is filled in. When all sections of the design are finished, fill in the background. Figure 7 shows a goose egg on which the flowers were worked in three shades of pink floss. The background is white. The hen's egg in Figure 7 is covered in black and white. The offset effect is created by beginning and ending each stripe at a planned point as part of the overall design.

FIGURE 7 Goose and hen's eggs covered with embroidery floss.

PLATE 16 Eggs can be decorated in any style or for any mood.

Mrs. F. R. Lawson

PLATE 17 Colors and trims are selected to complement window egg
figurines.

PLATE 18 Yellow enamel goose-egg box trimmed with white lace and
pearls and lined with white velvet. Gold-leafed box egg is
jewelled with No. 8 crystal and ruby rhinestones.

PLATE 19   The door on this fabulous egg opens to reveal an angel. The lid conceals a watch set in the top.

PLATE 20   Three fabulous hens' eggs.

PLATE 21   Watch egg. The miniature painting on a stand fits inside the egg.

Ideas for Embroidery-Floss Eggs

1. Use two shades of green and two shades of blue to make stripes in varying widths around the entire egg.
2. Instead of winding the floss around the egg crosswise, wind the floss on a diagonal. Make stripes of several shades. Start with the longest part of the diagonal. You will finish with a tight oval on each side of the egg.

Yarn

Lightweight yarn can be used in stripes on an egg. It is applied in the same way as embroidery floss. Try baby yarn and angora types as well.

Yarn flowers can be made by holding a length of yarn between the thumb and the index finger. Wind the yarn around itself until you have made a tight, flat circle. Shape this into an oval and glue it flat on the egg. For large daisies, make an oval for each petal. Leave the white eggshell as a background.

Feathers

Lovely eggs are made with a covering of small millinery feathers. Purchase feathers at a millinery supply shop or dismantle an old hat. Use feathers that are uniform in size and color. Cover one part of the egg at a time with Duco cement or a cement recommended for use with feathers. Start at one end of the egg and lay the feathers on in rows so that each row partially overlaps the preceding one like shingles on a roof.

Try covering an egg with one or two large feathers or plumes. Coat the entire egg with white glue. Gently roll the egg across the feather. The shell will show through the feather in a pattern. A feather was used to line the egg and the door in Figure 20. See page 60 for details.

String

A textured, antique look is produced by covering an egg with lengths of string glued on in patterns. Such an egg, finished with silver spray paint, is shown in Plate 2. On hens' eggs use white crocheting cotton, No. 61. A slightly heavier cord may be used on larger eggs. Lightly pencil the design onto the clean shell. Coat one part of the shell at a time with white glue and lay the cord on the penciled outline. Do not cross the string over itself. Cut where necessary. Keep the fingers free of glue. When the glue has dried, spray-paint the egg with several coats of enamel.

These eggs can be antiqued with Rub'n Buff or an antiquing glaze. To make your own antiquing glaze, thin a small amount of burnt sienna oil paint in turpentine. Brush it on the egg, leave it a few minutes, and wipe off any excess. Black or brown cream shoe polish is an excellent antiquing glaze. Spread the shoe polish with a soft cloth and partially wipe it off before it dries completely. Try black shoe polish on an egg sprayed silver, and brown shoe polish on an egg sprayed gold. Protect all antiquing glazes with a coat of fixative.

Instead of cotton cord, try covering an egg with cotton tatting, braid, or sturdy cotton lace. Apply the lace in rows as described. When the glue has dried, spray-paint the entire egg and antique it.

Use fabric braids that have a conspicuous texture. Try covering an egg with metallic braid such as silver rickrack and antiquing it with shoe polish.

Beads

An egg completely encrusted with glass or plastic beads makes a dazzling tree ornament. Use plastic cooking crystals, available in craft supply stores, small glass or plastic beads, opaque seed beads, or rocailles (very small beads).

Lightly pencil the design onto the egg. A simple, undetailed design is best. Spread the beads out on a plate or a piece of white paper. Spread glue on a small section of the design with a toothpick or hatpin and transfer the beads, one at a time, to the egg with a piece of kneading eraser. Avoid using excessive amounts of glue which will dull the beads. Each bead should touch the preceding one. The final result is more attractive if all the beads are arranged in parallel rows. Bead the design and then fill in the background.

Beads may be strung on fine nylon thread and wound onto the shell. Glue down one row of threaded beads at a time, trying not to spiral around the shell.

A quicker way to achieve a similar result is to coat the egg completely with glue and then roll it in a shallow bowl filled with beads. For this method to be successful, very small beads or small cooking crystals are essential.

An egg may be entirely covered or lined with sequins. Coat part of the egg at a time with glue and position the sequins with a kneading eraser. Try a goose egg sequined in a paisley design.

Ideas for Beaded Eggs
1. Working with cooking crystals, make large triangles or diamonds in one color and fill in the background with another. Plate 2 shows a hen's egg covered with cooking

PLATE 22 Gold-leafed egg holds a reproduction of Queen Elizabeth's coronation coach.

Mary Sammartino

PLATE 24 Diamond-studded egg opens to reveal a tiny bust of David.
Mary Sammartino

Mary Sammartino

PLATE 23 Circus egg with one door open.

FIGURE 8 Goose egg cut as a box and trim-
         med with tissue-paper flowers.

crystals. Make flower designs in red and green with glass or
plastic beads. Fill in the background with blue beads.

2. Using seed beads, copy the geometric designs used in
    Indian bead belts.

3. Cover an egg with sequins and top each sequin with a
    single bead. Try red beads on gold sequins and gold beads
    on red sequins in an overall pattern.

4. Paint an egg with enamel and cover it with translucent
    beads or sequins.

Tissue-Paper Collage

Use craft tissue papers in several harmonious colors to cover an
egg with a collage. Tear the paper into very small pieces and
smooth them onto an egg coated with white glue. The papers
are overlapped at the edges to blend the colors. When the egg is
entirely covered and the glue has dried, apply several coats of
clear shellac, spray lacquer, or a porcelain finish.

Ideas for Tissue-Paper Collage

1. Plate 2 shows two eggs completely covered with torn
    pieces of tissue paper. One uses red, yellow, pink, and
    lavender pieces. The other is done in blue, green, light
    blue, aquamarine, and purple.

2. Try cutting multicolored triangles of tissue paper and
    gluing them on the egg in a harlequin pattern.

3. Figure 8 shows a goose egg trimmed with tissue-paper
    flowers. Cut the egg so that the bottom is larger than the
    top and paint the shell with light blue acrylic paint. Each
    petal and leaf is cut separately from several colors of
    paper. Coat the entire surface with glue and position the
    pieces of paper with forceps. Give the tissue paper one or
    two coats of glue and two coats of lacquer. Trim the
    outside edges with silver braid.

COVERED AND JEWELLED EGGS

4. Tissue-paper butterflies are very attractive. Make the patterns on the wings by putting layers of one color paper on top of another.
5. Glue tissue paper over metallic paint and lacquer the egg.
6. Coat tissue-paper eggs with pale pastel nail polish instead of clear lacquer.

Fake Leather

Cut brown wrapping paper into ¼-inch squares. Glue the squares in rows around the egg. Use a pencil line to help keep the rows straight. Slightly overlap the squares. Outline each square lightly with lead pencil. Coat the entire egg with orange shellac to give the appearance of leather. Let the egg dry well before handling.

Découpage

Many découpage effects can be achieved by simply cutting out pictures and gluing them on an egg or by imitating formal découpage methods. Découpage under a porcelainlike finish is one of the most elegant egg decorations.

Magazines often have illustrations suitable for découpage: nosegays, cupids, Victorian pictures, etc. Antique papers are available from mail-order houses and craft stores. Gift-wrap paper and greeting cards are often sources of delightful seasonal cutouts. Because some printing inks smear when covered with lacquer, be sure to test the paper before you use it on your eggs.

The material should be carefully cut with sharp, delicate scissors to produce a beveled edge. Several papers can be overlapped as in collage. Work out the design before transferring the papers to the egg. Clip or tear the edges of the papers in inconspicuous places to help them assume the curves of the egg. Pour out a small amount of white glue onto a lid and spread it evenly and completely over the paper with a brush or toothpick. Smooth the paper onto the egg carefully, pressing out any air bubbles and making sure that all edges are glued down. Wipe up any excess glue with a moist cotton swab. Trapped air bubbles can be pricked with a pin and smoothed out.

After the paper and glue are completely dry, découpage pictures can be blended into the background color with pastel chalks. Select a color that blends with the cutout picture. Rub the chalk on a piece of fine sandpaper and transfer the dust to the egg with your finger, smoothing it around the edges of the picture and blending it into the design. Spray the egg immediately with at least two coats of fixative. Add gold trims after the first coat of fixative.

Découpage pictures can be sprayed with one or two coats of lacquer to keep them from smearing or they can be given a porcelainlike finish. They can also be given eight to ten coats of clear varnish. Go over the egg lightly with steel wool between each coat of varnish.

Ideas for Découpage Eggs

1. Plate 6 shows a goose egg painted black. Scenic pictures cut from a magazine were glued in place and the entire egg was given a porcelain finish. It was trimmed with gold paper and jewels, and a stand was fashioned from coat-hanger wire.

2. Use antique papers or old-fashioned pictures cut from magazines. Frame them with ovals of gold or silver papers. Give the egg several coats of varnish.

3. Cut out nursery-rhyme pictures and glue them onto brightly painted eggs. Spray the eggs with glossy lacquer. Make a mobile of these eggs for a child.

4. Découpage cutouts from gift-wrap paper onto eggs that have been given a coat of metallic spray paint. Finish with spray lacquer.

5. The goose egg in Figure 9 was sprayed gold and decorated with cutouts from flocked contact paper. The stand is a cube of wood covered with the same paper.

6. Cut out small reproductions of famous paintings and glue them on eggs. Frame them with gold paper.

7. Cut flowers from seed catalogs to glue on eggs (Plate 8).

8. Figure 10 shows a goose egg tinted with pale pink chalk. Gold cupids are glued over the chalk. Hang the egg with a

FIGURE 9 Goose egg on a pedestal covered with cutouts from flocked contact paper.

FIGURE 10 Goose egg with a découpage cupid, and hen's egg with a comic-strip cutout.

loop of deep-rose velvet ribbon on gold paper. The smaller hen's egg in Figure 10 is decorated with cutouts from a comic strip.

Adhesive-Backed Paper and Tape

Several kinds of decorative adhesive-backed tapes can be used to produce a handsome egg quickly and easily. Figure 11 shows an egg trimmed with diagonal stripes of black electrician's tape. The stand is a cube of wood covered with the same material. Cut patterns from adhesive-backed papers and create egg designs with them.

Dried Flowers and Pressed Butterflies

Dried, pressed flowers can be glued to a white egg or to an egg lightly tinted with chalk (Figure 12). Select small, flat-pressed flowers and ferns. Spring wild flowers, phlox, violets, tiny autumn leaves, single petals, and tansy leaves are all suited to this technique. Press the flowers for about a week by placing them between sheets of paper toweling in a heavy catalog or under several books. Be sure the flowers are completely dry before gluing them to the egg.

Arrange the blossoms and foliage on a piece of paper in plantlike arrangements. Apply white glue to the egg, *never* to the flowers. Using forceps, transfer the plant material to the egg one piece at a time. Press it firmly into the glue with the handle of a paintbrush. Do not stroke it or try to move it. The flowers will tear very easily. Carefully clean up any excess glue. Spray the egg with several coats of fixative as soon as the glue is dry. The coats of lacquer should build up a layer thick enough to protect the plant material from damage when the egg is handled. If a spray of blossoms is glued to either side of the egg, the shell can be circled with narrow velvet ribbon, leaving a loop at the top to serve as a hanger.

Pressed butterflies are available in craft supply stores. Although difficult to protect against scratching and tearing, they are so lovely that they're worth your efforts. They can be combined with the pressed ferns and flowers (Figure 12).

Select small butterflies and spread them out on a piece of paper. Handle them as little as possible and always with forceps. These butterflies usually have paper bodies attached to real wings and are best grasped by the body.

Coat the outside of the egg with white glue, but *never* attempt to spread glue on the butterflies. With the forceps, position the butterflies on the egg. They cannot be shifted once

FIGURE 11 Egg decorated with diagonal stripes of black electrician's tape.

FIGURE 12 Pressed flowers and butterflies make beautiful trims on eggs.

they are in place. With the handle of a paintbrush gently pat down any parts that do not lie flat. Do not stroke them because the wings will tear and the scales rub off easily. When the glue is completely dry, spray the egg with at least six coats of lacquer to protect the butterflies.

Ideas for Flower- and Butterfly-Covered Eggs

1. Use ferns and wild pinks, and loop the egg with a pink grosgrain ribbon. Or use ferns and violets with a violet velvet ribbon. Combine wild blue phlox and blue ribbon.
2. Use single petals from daisies and roses combined with dried tansy foliage.
3. Use tiny, brightly colored autumn leaves. Small Japanese maple leaves are excellent.
4. Combine several small pressed pansies and a single butterfly.
5. Scatter several different butterflies around an egg and place bits of tansy or fern between them.

JEWELLED EGGS

Eggs trimmed with pearls, rhinestones, other imitation jewels, and gold papers are the aristocrats of decorated eggs. They may be pendant eggs, window eggs, or jewel-box eggs. Découpage finishes, some paints, pastels, and metallic gold and silver spray finishes harmonize best with jewels and gold trims. Metal-flake paints and pastel porcelainlike finishes make exquisite formal settings for jewels and gold papers. Découpage papers and cameos framed in gold paper have a special place in jewelled eggs. Gold leaf, too, can be applied to the eggshell.

Supplies

Mail-order firms which supply jewel trims are listed in the Appendix. Fabric stores, bridal shops, dime stores, hobby shops, and department stores sell imitation jewels, metallic braids, tiny hinges, and sequins. Jewels labeled "flat-backed" or "boutique" are faceted on one side and flat on the other to facilitate gluing. Select an assortment of colors, sizes, and shapes as well as some bugles (long, narrow beads) rocailles, pearlized collars and ringlets. Spherical, flat-backed, and oat-seed shaped pearls are available. They can be obtained without holes from Jewel Creations. These, and old yellowed pearls from costume jewelry, can be dyed with fabric dye in many exciting colors. Follow the directions on the package, removing the pearls from the dye when the desired color intensity has been reached. Rinse them in cool water and spray them with fixative.

You can buy costume jewelry on sale and cut it apart to provide trims. You can also buy and cut apart gold filigree findings used for jewelry-making. Cut the shanks from fancy buttons, stickpins, and hatpins.

You will want a collection of gold lace papers. These are the heavy, embossed papers sold for découpage which are available in border designs, in oval frames, as medallions, and in such specific motifs as bows and lettering. To begin, select two or three narrow border trims and one large medallion or set of ovals which you can cut up into small pieces.

These gold papers can be silvered by wiping them with fingernail polish remover. Light wiping produces an antique silver; more wiping yields a bright silver. Both the gold and silver should be protected against tarnishing with a coat of clear finish.

Experiment by cutting gold papers into various shapes and rearranging them. Keyholes with the centers cut out make very nice frames for large jewels. Rosettes, snowflakes, stars, scrolls, oval frames, daguerrotype frames, and escutcheons combined with jewels and pearls create unique eggs.

Have on hand a few gold and silver fabric braids and lengths of ¼-inch velvet ribbon in several colors. A yard of each color is sufficient. To keep braids from raveling at the cut ends, touch them with a drop of white glue or clear nail polish. Many metallic braids combine gold or silver with colored threads and effectively pick up colors used elsewhere in the egg.

For directions on making tiny hinges and latches, see page 49.

Directions

When you create a jewelled egg, work out the design and color scheme in advance. The shape of the cuts, the lining, the colors, the texture of the finish, and the choice of trim should all be harmonious.

Cut and clean the egg and put on the finish. Fix the finish with one coat of clear spray. Complete the inside of box and window eggs. Gold papers and jewels are usually added last after all the other work is complete.

Select a group of stones and pearls in colors that complement the finish of the egg. Lay out the stones and gold papers in the exact design you want on a piece of white paper or a china plate. Before the jewels are added, the gold papers are glued in place and the whole egg is sprayed with two or more coats of lacquer or fixative. Gold papers must be clipped at intervals when they are applied around curves in the design. If many curves are involved in the design, it may be helpful to substitute gold braid.

The jewels are applied last because additional coats of lacquer tend to dull them. With a toothpick or hatpin, put a drop of glue on the egg and position the jewels one at a time on the glue with a piece of kneadable eraser or jeweler's wax. Be careful not to get excess glue on the jewels. White glue is perfectly satisfactory for gluing stones, but epoxy glues, although harder to use, have greater holding power on small stones that can be dislodged easily.

Most craftsmen prefer not to combine sequins and jewels, although a sequin mounted under a rhinestone sometimes will give the stone greater sparkle.

Both Austrian and German rhinestones are available. Austrian machine-cut stones are more expensive but have greater sparkle than the German stones, which are mostly die-formed and therefore not as brilliant.

Gold Leaf

Gold leaf is easy to apply and is much more beautiful than gold paint. Select a quick-drying gold leaf medium such as Hasting's Quick Dry. Apply the medium to a clean, dry, unpainted egg. Always work with gold leaf on a dry day. A little practice is necessary to determine when the medium is ready. If it loses the leaf, it is too dry. If it eats the leaf, it is too moist; if this happens, let it dry, apply more medium over the leaf and try again. The medium should feel tacky but not sticky. On a dry day it takes about one hour to dry sufficiently.

Roll the prepared egg across the leaf. With clean, dry fingers or a flannel cloth, smooth the leaf over the ends of the egg and brush off the excess. Use a soft brush to pick up small pieces of leaf and touch them down onto uncovered spots. Gently buff the leaf with a clean velour powder puff or a soft flannel cloth until the seams disappear.

Apply leaf to stands, cupids, hinges, etc., in the same way. Use a small, soft, dry brush to transfer small pieces of leaf into cracks and hard-to-reach recesses. Use the brush to smooth the leaf down.

Pendants

Whole eggs, exquisitely gilded, jewelled, and suspended with nylon monofilament fishline make marvelous Christmas tree ornaments; but they are so beautiful that you may want to use them all year round. The uncut egg allows great freedom in the use of trims. Work out the design with gold papers — perhaps framing a tiny painting or a cameo. Finish the bottom of the egg with a pendant jewel or a series of collars and jewels such as filigree balls and teardrop pearls.

Try tassels instead of pendant jewels. The tassel in Figure 23 was made from an earring. Purchase drapery tassels or make your own of metallic thread. Wind the thread many times around a piece of cardboard. Slip the loops off, knot them tightly at one end, and cut the loops at the other. Glue the tassel in place.

The top of the pendant egg is finished with metal filigree findings, collars, circular bits of gold paper, and jewels. Fishline is threaded through the holes that were used to blow out the egg, and glued at both ends, leaving a loop at the top. Bring the loop through the trims at the top of the egg as they are glued in place.

FIGURE 13 Elegantly jewelled pendant eggs.

Ideas for Pendant Eggs

Yellow Tree Ornament (Figure 13). Give a whole, blown goose egg a yellow porcelainlike finish. Circle the egg lengthwise with lacy gold braid. Make a top by gluing two pearl collars together. Glue a large pearl into the upper collar. The bottom is a crystal pendant jewel in a pearl collar. Small pearls ring the jewel in the collar. Glue a nylon fishline hanger in position. Trim the opposite faces of the egg with a sunburst design worked in ruby teardrop boutique jewels, silver bugles, and a gold and crystal sunburst mounted on a gold-paper keyhole so that the hole is covered. (See also Plates 3 and 8.)

Green Jewelled Ornament (Figure 13). Apply a pale green porcelain finish to a whole, blown hen's egg. Ring it with gold paper slightly above its equator. Trim the top of the egg with six lengths of gold cord and the bottom with two lengths of gold paper. Glue a pearl on the bottom. Glue a pearl in a pearl collar to the top, and glue a loop of gold cord into the collar for a hanger. Jewel the egg with emerald stones and silver bugles.

COVERED AND JEWELLED EGGS

4

JEWEL-BOX EGGS

The jewel-box egg is cut so that it can be opened and closed. These eggs can hold a surprise, as did so many of the Imperial Russian Easter eggs, or they can hold some small treasure. The larger eggs, especially goose eggs, are very effective when made into boxes and are useful to hold small pieces of jewelry.

The eggs can be cut lengthwise or crosswise. They may be cut so that one side is larger than the other. The cutting line may be scalloped or fluted; the lid, hinged or fitted.

Any finish can be used on these eggs but the more elegant ones are most successful. The boxes are often decorated with gold or silver papers, velvet ribbon, braids, fake jewels, pearls, and beads. These eggs must have a stand or pedestal. Often they have a handle, latches, hinges, or pulls. Tiny brass latches and hinges are available where découpage supplies are sold.

See the list of suggested household items that can be used for pedestals on page 9. The pedestal is added as other trims are added, and secured with white glue. The curve of the shell can be joined to the flat top of the pedestal with a piece of gold paper or a ring of braid. Jewelling should be planned so that the design helps to make the transition from pedestal to egg.

HINGES
Box eggs can be hinged with a tiny brass hinge glued to the outside of the shell after all other trimming is finished. You can

custom-make your own tiny hinges and latches with pointed scissors. Cut them from the metal ends of juice cans, shape them with jeweler's pliers. Gold-leaf or paint them. The pin in these hinges can be made from a dress pin.

A more functional hinge, however, is made with a piece of elastic glued to the interior of the egg and concealed under a lining. Use the flat 3/8 inch wide elastic sold for repairing waistbands. For a goose egg, cut two pieces of elastic each about 1½ inches long. Glue one end of each piece side by side on the inside back of the bottom half of the shell. Line that half of the shell and let the hinge dry overnight. Then glue the other ends of the two elastic strips to the center back of the top shell so that, when closed, the two halves of the shell come together. Line the second half. Finish the inside top edges of the lining with lace or gold braid which will hide the hinge and the top edge of the lining.

Unlined eggs may be hinged with one or two strips of ¼-inch velvet ribbon applied, after the inside of the egg has been painted, in the same way as the elastic. The inside top edge of the shell may be trimmed with braid to hide the ends of the velvet ribbon. Velvet is not as sturdy as elastic and will not wear as well. Lids and doors can be anchored with a short length of fine chain as well (Plate 9).

Small decorative hangers designed to screw into a piece of wood can be used as handles on eggs. The screw section is cut off with heavy wire cutters or a hacksaw. Large jewels, buttons, beads, and loops of velvet ribbon and soutache will make lifts and handles on box eggs. Tiny brass latches, sold with découpage supplies, are suitable on larger eggs. All metal findings should be coated with lacquer and glued to the finished egg.

INTERIORS

The inside of the egg should be finished to complement the outside. It may be left white and lacquered, painted with enamels, metallic paints, or pastel chalks. Try coating the inside of the shell with white glue and then dusting it with glitter. Shake out the excess. Tinted paraffin makes a lovely lining for boxes. White gold leaf is beautiful lining for gold-leafed eggs.

Interior finishes should be completed at the same time that the outside finish is completed and before the gold papers and jewels are added.

A fabric lining gives an especially luxurious look to an egg, particularly one that is to hold small pieces of jewelry. Be sure the outside of the egg can be handled without being damaged by fingerprints. It is best to jewel the egg after it is lined because the stones are easily dislodged during handling.

On the outside, the cut edges of the shell should be concealed with gold paper or braid. Allow the braid to extend about 1/16 inch beyond the edge of the shell. This will conceal the edge of the lining and the braid inside without interfering with the egg's closing.

When an egg is wider than it is deep (Figure 14), use a soft, drapeable fabric such as rayon velvet, cotton, lace, or silk as a lining. Cut a rectangle of cloth larger than the shell half. Coat the inside of the egg with white glue. Position the fabric, starting at the center bottom. Working carefully with the fingers, smooth it toward the edges, avoiding pleats and wrinkles. Some small gathers are inevitable at the top edge of the egg, but most can be smoothed out of a soft fabric. The rest can be covered with a fabric trim around the inside edge of the shell.

As you work, cut away excess fabric. Use a toothpick to slip glue under the top edge of the fabric, making sure that the edges are securely fastened down. Allow the lining to dry while working on the other half of the shell. Trim the edge carefully with small scissors.

Finish the inside top edge with lace, braid, or ribbon, putting the glue on the ribbon one section at a time. Roll the edge of the ribbon slightly to cover the edge of the lining and the raw edge of the shell. You may have to hold the ribbon in place until it is partly dry.

A bow can be tied separately and glued to the inside back of the box to conceal the ends of the ribbon. Avoid getting glue on the fabric. A small amount can be wiped off with a damp cotton swab. Since glue will show through lace and very thin fabrics, line these materials with a lightweight cotton, cutting, positioning, and gluing both layers of material simultaneously.

When the egg box is deeper than it is wide, the fabric can be draped in a series of graceful folds inside the shell. Cut a square of fabric larger than the shell half. Coat the inside of the shell with white glue. Starting at the center of the shell, smooth the fabric into a series of equal folds that spiral slightly from the center to the edge of the shell. At the center bottom, the fabric will tend to bunch up. It can be clipped a little if necessary. Cover a small circle of cardboard with fabric and glue it in the center bottom of the egg to hide the clipped area; or use a large button or jewel for this purpose. Finish the top edge with braid.

Stiff fabrics such as satin and brocade will not respond to the inner curve of the shell so pieces of lightweight cardboard are inserted to simplify the shape. This method is more formal

FIGURE 14 A large egg box will hold small pieces of jewelry.

than the preceding one. Cut an oval of cardboard to fit the bottom of the egg. This will form the flat base of the box which you are constructing inside the egg shell. Next cut a strip of cardboard long enough to go around the edge of the shell. Make it wide enough to form the sides of the box. Join the ends to form a ring. Fit this ring around the inside edge of the shell and glue the ends together. Make any necessary adjustments in the shape of the cardboard pieces. It is wise to cut these pieces first as a paper pattern, making all adjustments before cutting them in cardboard.

Using the cardboard as a pattern, cut a fabric oval ¼ inch larger than the cardboard. Coat the cardboard lightly with white glue and center the fabric on it. Clip the overhanging edges of fabric at intervals, turn them under, and glue them to the wrong side.

Cut another strip of fabric ¼ inch wider than the cardboard strip and glue it to the cardboard strip in the same way, turning the extra fabric to the back and gluing it. Glue both covered pieces of cardboard into position in the egg. Finish the outside and top edge of the shell with gold paper or braid.

To make a ring stand inside a box egg, cut a block of styrofoam 1" x 1" x 1½". Cut a V-shaped groove across it. Cover the styrofoam with the same material as the lining and glue the block into the center of the box to hold the ring.

Ideas for Jewel-Box Eggs

Pink Lace Box (Figure 14). Cut a goose egg in half and spray-paint it with pale pink enamel. Cover both the top and the bottom with ½ inch wide white ribbon lace. The edges are finished with narrow, rose velvet ribbon. Both the stand and the top pull are small bottle caps covered with rose velvet ribbon. The egg is trimmed with pearls, pink beads from a necklace, silver bugles, and one red, rose-shaped button. To make pearl loops that hang from the bottom half of the egg, string several pearls on a thread and glue only the ends of the thread to the egg. The egg is lined with white velvet over an elastic hinge. The inside edge is finished with white tatting.

Red and White Box (Plate 5 and Figure 15). Cut a goose egg in half crosswise; flute the edges. Give it a white porcelainlike finish. Divide the egg into six sections. Glue six lengths of narrow velvet ribbon to both the top and bottom of the egg so that when the halves are together the velvet ribbon appears to be continuous. Trim the cut edge of the top half with gold braid. (The braid used here has a red thread woven in with the gold.) The top is a gold filigree cap with a ruby stone. The stand is made by gluing four pearl collars together. Trim the front, as shown, with ruby boutique stones, both teardrops and round; ruby bugles; and a crystal pendant. The central jewel is a red glass button. The pendant is glued to the top half of the egg under the button. Cut part of the shank off the button if necessary, and mount it on a pearl ring to make it more secure. Paint the inside of the egg with white enamel.

Pink Porcelain Box (Plate 4). Pencil a fluted cutting line on a goose egg. Reinforce it with tape and cut with a razor blade. Paint the egg with pale pink acrylic paint. Pink often bleeds, so coat the paint with fixative before giving it a porcelainlike finish with glue. Paint the inside with rose enamel. Trim the cut edge of the top with a narrow gold-border paper, clipping the paper to make it follow the curves of the cut edges. Glue an oval frame of gold paper to the top of the lid. Spray the shell with gloss lacquer. Finish the top with crystal and pink rhinestones, oat-shaped pearls, and seed pearls. Spray a length of the same gold-border paper with gloss fixative and let it dry. Glue a narrow rose velvet ribbon around the cut edge of the bottom half. Clip a tiny triangle out of the ribbon at the points of the curves. Glue these clipped edges down securely (always butt-join ribbon; never overlap it). Glue the sprayed gold paper around the edge of the ribbon, clipping where necessary. Glue three large pearls in place for feet. Allow the egg to dry overnight. Glue a small brass catch to the top and bottom.

FIGURE 15 Jewelled goose-egg box with velvet stripes.

Green Porcelain Egg (Plate 4). Cut a goose egg in half and paint it inside and out with pale green acrylic paint. Give both the inside and outside a porcelainlike finish with glue. Glue a border of gold paper ½ inch wide around the cut edge of the top half of the shell so that it extends beyond the edge. The bottom half of the shell will fit inside this strip of paper when the egg is complete. Glue gold metallic cord on the center of the gold paper. The cord used here has red and green threads interwoven with the gold. Glue a gold paper frame to the top of the egg. Make a ring of gold paper, clipping both edges. Glue the ring to both a pearlized daisy stand and to the egg. Spray the egg with gloss lacquer. Complete the trim with round and teardrop boutique emerald rhinestones, green bugles, and one central pearl.

Blue Metallic Box (Plate 6). Cut a goose egg in half and paint it blue with metal-flake enamel. Rub a strip of gold paper with a piece of cotton soaked in nail-polish remover until the paper turns silver. Glue the paper around the cut edge of the top half of the shell so that it overlaps the bottom half slightly. The two large pieces of trim on this egg are part of a costume-jewelry necklace. Jewelry can be cut up into suitably sized pieces with pliers or tin snips. The top pull is a large pearl glued into a small pearl collar. Light blue jewels are glued onto 12 mm. silver spangles and ringed with small pearl frames. The pedestal is a wooden drawer pull painted to match the egg. The bottom half of the egg is trimmed with silver paper, silver bugles, pearls, and the same spangle-jewel-pearl ring motif that is used on the top. The inside of the egg is painted silver.

Hen's Egg with a Lid (Figure 16). Cut off the top third from the rounded end of a hen's egg. Paint the egg with pale blue acrylic paint and give it a porcelainlike finish. The stand is a small pearl collar. The top is trimmed with a filigree cap with a central blue stone. Trim the cut edge of both the lid and the bottom with gold paper. Pieces of a gold-paper medallion are cut to resemble handles and latches and glued on. Pearl clusters are added as desired.

Egg Trunk Trim the outside of this egg with brown paper coated with orange shellac to imitate leather. Cut strips from gold gift-wrap paper and brush them with shoe polish to antique them. Attach them to resemble brass fittings. Handles are made from brass plaque hangers with the screw section removed. Line the egg with antique paper to resemble an old steamer trunk. Glue four small brass balls in place for feet.

FIGURE 16 Hen's egg box trimmed with gold découpage papers.

5

WINDOW EGGS

Window eggs have an opening cut in the shell so that a figure or scene inside is visible   These elaborately jewelled, painted, or covered eggs either hang, stand on pedestals, stand upright or on one side. A single figure, such as a ceramic animal or tiny doll, can be mounted inside the egg, or a complete scene can be carefully scaled to fit inside the shell.

Plan the shape of the opening on paper and transfer it to the egg with pencil. The window may be oval, rectangular, or round. It can be scalloped or arched. Try a heart-shaped opening for a Valentine egg. A grillwork window can be created with liquid solder. Think of the shape of the opening as a frame for the objects inside. Try making several windows, or one in front and one in back. If multiple openings are planned, or if most of the egg is to be cut away, the shell should be hardened or reinforced with transparent tape before it is cut.

If the shell is cut with a power tool or a razor blade, the piece removed will remain intact and can be mounted as a door or as shutters on the window (Figures 20 and 26). Such a door can be glued, or hinged in the same way as box eggs. Sometimes a door mounted to stand open will throw the finished egg out of balance. This can be corrected with a piece of lead shot concealed inside. Drop the piece of lead inside the egg and stand the egg upright. The lead will shift around to a position that will balance the egg. When it has positioned itself, secure it with a drop of glue and hide it among the interior decorations.

Pedestals suitable for window eggs are discussed on page 8. Use a piece of gold paper or braid to make a smooth transition from the flat top of the pedestal to the bottom of the rounded egg.

There are many small figures and animals suitable for the inside of eggs. Some of these are sold by mail-order houses. Stores which carry scale model electric trains will have many tiny accessories suitable for eggs, and some doll house accessories are small enough for use in eggs. Try building accessories of balsa wood and glue. Large toy stores have tiny people, animals, musical instruments, etc. Items sold as party favors are often in the proper scale for decorated eggs. Small ceramic figures found in gift shops and antique shops are charming when mounted in window eggs.

Round and oval wooden beads and matchsticks can be glued together to make people and animals. The round beads become heads; the oval beads, bodies; the matchsticks, limbs. Paint the figures with acrylic paints using a No. 000 brush for the tiniest features. Spray with fixative. These figures are delightful when used to carry out a nursery-rhyme or a children's-story motif. A cat can be made from two beads glued together and painted. Make the ears of paper; the tail, from a piece of wire. Make a bride from two beads and bits of tulle or net. An angel can be created from a bead and paper cone. Cut wings and glue them in place.

The outside of window eggs should set off the interior just as a frame sets off a picture. For example, a beautifully jewelled exterior will enhance a tiny porcelain ballerina mounted inside. Small pieces of dried fern and violets on the outside will blend with a woodland gnome. Hand-painted angels under a por-celainlike finish complement an angel inside.

Plan both the inside and outside at the same time. You will find it is easiest to trim both simultaneously. Let the glue and paint dry completely at each stage. On the inside of the egg, the background and the floor are finished before the figures are positioned. Small foreground figures and bushes are added last.

The interior decorations should accent the central figure rather than overwhelm it. Completely lining an egg with silver beads may be the perfect setting for a ceramic ballerina, but a delicate wood carving needs only the sculptured white curve of the shell. A few well-placed sequins or a light dusting of chalk may be all the inside of the egg needs. Simplicity is often most successful.

Eggs can be lined with the angel hair used on Christmas trees. If this material is not available, use similar material sold in fish stores for use as aquarium filters. Select a brand that doesn't contain glass fibers. Coat the inside of the shell with glue and lightly place the angel hair in position. This is a perfect background for a gold Christmas angel. Add a few gold sequins or glitter.

Window eggs can be lined with fabric or lace in the same manner as that described for lining jewel-box eggs on page 50. A large feather glued inside the egg makes a handsome lining (Figure 20).

Lining an egg with paraffin will give it a silky translucence. Melt ordinary canning paraffin or candlewax over water. Make a pouring spout by pinching the lip of a clean tin can. Put the wax in the can and stand the can in boiling water. Add small pieces of wax crayon to color the wax. When the wax has completely melted, stir it to mix in the color and carefully pour a small amount into the egg. Roll the egg so that the hot wax coats the entire inside. Any excess can be poured out or allowed to pool in the bottom. Build up several coats of wax if you like. When the wax is partially set, position any figures that are to stand in it. The wax will hold them securely without glue.

As the background is completed, the floor on which the three-dimensional figures will stand is inserted. The floor can be made with sand poured into the bottom of the shell and mixed well with a thin solution of white glue and water. If sand makes the shell too heavy, vermiculite or kitty litter can be used in the same way. Bits of styrofoam or corrugated cardboard painted or covered with fabric can be cut to fit the inside bottom of the shell. Platforms or stages can be made with cardboard so that one group of figures is elevated. Glass percolator tops make almost invisible stands inside an egg.

Melted paraffin can be pooled in the bottom of the shell and figures mounted in it while it is still soft. Snow inside an egg can be made with paraffin. Melt untinted paraffin over water. When it is completely melted, let it stand until a scum appears on the top of the hot wax. Then beat it with a hand egg beater until it has formed a thick white foam. With a fork, transfer the foam to the inside of the egg. Sprinkle it with glitter while it is still warm; mount any figures in it before it cools (Figure 29).

To create a complete scene in an egg, plan the scene in detail outside the shell, and transfer it one piece at a time. Forceps are helpful when inserting small items.

The background for a scenic egg is painted onto the inside back and sides. To bring painted material into partial relief, cut some pieces from shirtboard or lightweight cardboard and glue them into the back of the egg. Paint both cardboard and egg. For example, clouds may be painted on the shell, with stars and moon glued on; or walls can be painted with windows, and shutters glued on.

When the background work is finished, glue the figures in place. Two-dimensional cutouts can be glued to cardboard and glued into the shell or made to stand in warm paraffin. Three-dimensional figures are usually more effective. If several figures are used, carefully consider their scale in relation to each other. They do not all necessarily have to be the same size, but they should look right. The illusion of depth can be heightened by placing slightly smaller figures toward the back of the egg. Figures toward the back of the scene can be raised slightly above those in the foreground. Make one figure the focal point of the scene. Avoid overcrowding the egg as this confuses the eye.

Miniature Christmas tree lights may be mounted through the hole in the top of the shell to spotlight the inside. Seal them into position with epoxy. Be sure that all trims used inside the egg are fireproof. The heat from the bulb can ignite flammable materials.

Birds, angels, and girls on swings may also be hung from the top hole with nylon monofilament fishline so that they swing in the egg. Secure the fishline to the hole with white glue. Such eggs may need extra weight in the base to provide stability. Position lead shot in the egg or in the pedestal when necessary.

PLASTIC-WRAP WINDOWS

Some hobbyists cover the egg window with clear plastic used for wrapping food. Do this after the inside is completed and before the outside edge of the window is trimmed. Apply white glue to the edge of the window. Cut a piece of plastic wrap slightly larger than the window and stretch it tightly across the window. It must be taut. When the glue is dry, put the window side of the egg in boiling water for a few seconds. Trim off excess plastic wrap 3/8 inch from the edge of the window. Then glue decorative braid trim around the edge of the window to conceal the cut edges of plastic wrap.

Many hobbyists feel that plastic windows detract from the egg. You may want to try it and decide for yourself whether they suit your taste and style.

STAINED-GLASS WINDOWS

Windows that allow light to enter through a picture so that they resemble stained glass can be made in several ways.

Taylor House occasionally sells Italian silks on which copies of the Old Masters have been reproduced. Glue these into the back window of a multiple window egg so that the light shows through. Sheer silk dress fabrics with a suitable print may also be used. Try mounting a Christmas tree light inside such an egg so that the light shines out through the silk.

Another method of making stained-glass windows requires old Christmas cards. Cut out the picture you want to use and place it face down on the adhesive side of clear contact paper. Smooth it out. Soak the card and the contact paper in clear water until the paper softens. Carefully rub off all the wet paper, leaving the print on the contact. Mount as above.

Figure 17 shows a goose egg with a double window. The back window was filled with a Christmas card picture and the egg was sprayed gold inside and out. Both windows were trimmed with gold cord.

Translucent paper printed to resemble stained glass is often available at Christmas time. Some Christmas cards also have "stained glass" paper inserts.

Ideas for Window Eggs — Christmas

Select the figure or figures to go inside the egg and let them guide you in your choice of materials and colors. Follow these directions or let them guide you in designing your own egg.

Green Christmas Violinist (Figure 18). Cut an oval window in a goose egg. Paint the outside of the egg with green metal-flake paint. Leave the inside white, with membrane intact. Glue a 3/4 inch, square wooden drawer pull in place for a pedestal and paint it with the same enamel. Glue an oval frame of gold paper to the cut edge of the window. Allow the paper to flare out from the edge rather than gluing it down tightly. The figure itself is one of a set of paper musicians sold as Christmas tree ornaments. It can be copied easily with a paper cone painted and glued to a wooden bead. Use pipe cleaners for arms and make a violin of gold Christmas paper.

Christmas Angels (Figure 19 and Plate 10). The two goose eggs in Figure 19 and the green egg in Plate 10 contain easily made figures. Glue a wooden bead to a cone of construction paper. Paint the robe and face, using a very small brush. The lines on the robe are gold. The face is simply made of small dots: blue for the eyes, red for the mouth, and pale pink for the

FIGURE 17 Goose egg with double window and "stained-glass" madonna.

FIGURE 18 A goose egg trimmed in green, gold, and white.

By Mrs. F. R. Lawson

FIGURE 20 Wooden angel in a goose egg lined with a red feather.

FIGURE 19 Two easy-to-make Christmas tree angels.

cheeks. Practice making these simple faces on a piece of scrap paper. You will find them very easy to do. The hair is made by gluing on short strands of separated and unwound gold cord. Make wings in cardboard, paint them gold, and glue them to the back of the angel. In the egg on the left in Figure 19, the angel's robe is red. The egg is pale green enamel on the outside and white inside. It is trimmed with scattered spangles, and gold sequins which were bought by the yard. In the egg on the right, the angel's robe is pale blue. The outside of the egg is dark blue enamel trimmed in gold. A cloud of cotton surrounds the base of the angel.

Wooden Angel (Figure 20). The oval removed from this goose egg is used as a door. Spray silver on the inside of both the door and the egg; mask well, then spray gold on the outside of the egg and the door. The rims of both the door and the opening are trimmed with gold, red, and green braid. Glue the door so that it stands open. Stand the egg on a small pearl collar. Glue a small piece of balsa wood in the bottom of the egg to make a base for the angel. Coat the inside of the egg lightly with glue and line the egg and the balsa-wood base with a large red feather. The feather used here came from a child's Indian

FIGURE 21 Hen's egg nativity scene.

By Mrs. F. R. Lawson

FIGURE 22 Gold window goose egg with a Christmas lapel-pin angel.

headdress. The feather should not be pressed flat into the glue, but allowed to fluff around the angel. Line the door with part of another red feather. Glue the small wooden angel to the balsa-wood platform. If necessary, secure a small lead weight under the figure to balance the egg. Paint an angel on the outside back of the egg with red enamel.

Nativity Scene in Hen's Egg (Figure 21). Cut an oval from a hen's egg and paint the egg inside and out with robin's-egg blue acrylic paint. Give the outside of the egg a porcelainlike finish. Glue a cluster of pearls to the top and trim the rim of the window with gold paper. Clip the paper at frequent intervals. Cut a circle of cardboard for the stand and ring it with gold paper. Glue the stand to the egg.

Make a floor in the bottom of the egg with an oval of cardboard. Coat the inside of the egg with glue and line the egg with aquarium filter material or angel hair. Glue the three nativity figures in place on the cardboard floor. These figures can be assembled from small round and oval beads.

Lapel-Pin Angel (Figure 22). Cut an oval window in a goose egg. Spray the outside of the egg gold. Leave the inside white, with one layer of membrane intact. Trim the edge of the

WINDOW EGGS

window with gold braid. On the outside of the shell, trim down the center back, and down each side, with a red, green, and gold braid. Leave a loop of this braid at the top of the egg for a hanger.

The figure inside this egg is a Christmas lapel pin. Trim the egg to harmonize with the pin. Glue a fluff of white cotton into the egg around the base of the figure. Touch the cotton lightly with glue and sprinkle it with gold glitter.

Gold Angel in a Blue Egg (Figure 23 and Plate 10). Cut a large oval window in a goose egg. Paint the egg with blue enamel inside and out. Trim the rim of the window with gold braid. Space ½-inch gold spangles around the outside of the egg. Glue a blue jewel in the center of each spangle. At the top of the egg make a hanger from a loop of gold cord. Glue a circle of small pearls at the base of the gold cord. The pendant is made from an earring which has three pearls hanging from lengths of gold chain. Crumble a piece of dark velvet and glue it to the inside bottom. When the glue is dry, glue a gold angel in place on the velvet.

Gold Angel with Flowers (Figure 24). In this goose egg, simplicity is the secret of its success. The gold angel stands on white, crumpled velvet folded over a piece of styrofoam. Behind the angel is a piece of dried fern. Fabric flowers are glued in place at her feet. The outside of the egg is painted pale yellow and bands of sequins are used as trim around the window. Pearls mounted on large spangles are attached at intervals around the back of the egg. Also see Plate 17.

Nativity Scene in Large Egg (Figure 25). Cut an oval window in a large egg. Paint the outside with blue metal-flake enamel. Lay the egg on its side. Make a base from two layers of corrugated cardboard cut in ovals and glued together. Finish the edge of the stand with brown velvet.

Work out on paper the exact positions of the figures and make several cardboard platforms inside the egg to hold them on different levels. Before gluing the platforms in position, check to be sure that they and the figures will all fit in the egg as planned. Line the inside of the egg and cover the platforms with brown velvet. Finish the cut edge of the shell with gold cord. When the glue has dried overnight, use forceps to insert a few of the figures at a time. Let the glue on them dry before putting in the rest. Glue the angel to the inside top of the egg. Glue the star to the lip of the window. Place the largest animal on a stand made of velvet-covered cardboard beside the egg.

FIGURE 25 Nativity scene in a window goose egg.

FIGURE 26 It is possible to arrange an entire scene inside a large egg.

Christmas House (Figure 26 and Plate 11). Cut a semisquare door in a goose egg. Trim and paint the outside of the egg to resemble a house. Hinge the door in place. Glue a cardboard or balsa-wood chimney on the roof and dust the egg with artificial snow or whipped paraffin. Make a stand from a drawer pull or build front steps out of balsa wood.

Paint the inside of the egg to resemble walls. Make a fireplace of lightweight cardboard, and glue it to the back of the egg. Hang paper stockings on the mantel. Candles are cut from birthday-cake candles. Make a cardboard floor and paint or glue a rug on it. Stand a tiny Christmas tree inside the egg. It can be trimmed with glitter, sequins, beads, and a single strand of foil icicle. Make tiny balsa packages. The chair in this egg was made from balsa wood.

Velvet-Covered Egg (Figure 27). Harden a goose egg by brushing it with Duco cement. Draw four long, pointed ovals on the four sides of the egg. Cut the ovals out with a utility knife or razor blade. Paint the inside of the egg with medium-blue acrylic paint.

You will need a rectangle of velvet about twice as long and twice as wide as the egg. Estimate the amount needed by fitting a paper towel loosely over the egg and cutting it to shape as a pattern. Dark blue velvet was used on this egg.

FIGURE 27 Multiple windows in a goose egg covered in blue velvet.

WINDOW EGGS

FIGURE 28 Triptych egg.

Coat the top third of the egg with white glue. Center the rectangle of velvet on the top and smooth it down over the glued portion of the egg. Cut a slit in the velvet through the center of each oval window. Coat the second third of the egg — the arches between the windows — with glue. Smooth the fabric into place between the windows, cutting away excess material as you work, until the fabric is glued to the base of the windows. Smooth out all wrinkles.

Coat the rest of the egg with glue. On the bottom third of the egg, cut and fit two pieces of velvet so that there is a straight-line seam along the bottoms of the windows. Join the two pieces of velvet by making a seam from the bottom point of one window, through the center bottom of the egg, to the bottom point of the opposite window. Do not overlap the pieces of fabric. Butt the raw edges together and glue them down. One piece of fabric will smoothly cover an entire egg with seams only at the bottom if it is cut in this fashion. This will not work unless the egg has several windows cut in it.

Outline the windows inside and out with narrow, gold rickrack, covering the raw edges of fabric and shell. Coat the inside lightly with glue and dust it with gold glitter. Shake out the excess. Glue a glass percolator top face down on the inside bottom of the egg. Let it dry. Glue a gold angel on the percolator top.

Spray a one-inch wooden drawer pull with gold spray and fixative, and glue it to the bottom of the egg for a pedestal. Brush the velvet with a stiff brush to bring up the pile.

Triptych Egg (Figure 28 and Plate 12). Cut a goose egg in half, and then cut one of the halves lengthwise. Paint the egg old rose and glue découpage angels to the doors. All edges are trimmed with gold découpage papers and the egg is given a matte finish. Small brass hinges are glued in position with the doors closed. Hold them with a large rubber band until the glue dries. The doors will open and shut. The madonna is a relief figure supported by a square of balsa wood and surrounded with crumpled brown velvet.

Santa Tree Ornament (Plate 3). A hen's egg is made into a tree ornament by cutting a window and mounting inside a tiny Santa surrounded by cotton. The egg is left white, and trimmed with gold rickrack and a loop of red velvet ribbon.

Gold-Leafed Hens' Eggs with oval windows, trimmed with a single row of gold rickrack or gold cord and a loop of velvet (Plate 3), can be made in quantity. Inside each egg, mount a single small angel or Christmas figure. This simplicity of decoration is much more successful on smaller eggs than elaborate jewelling and complicated scenes. These simple eggs make very elegant tree ornaments.

Winter Scene (Figure 29). The size of a goose egg makes a more elaborate interior scheme possible. To avoid the appearance of overdecoration, the egg is planned in two colors, gold and white. The outside of the egg is coated with glue, sprinkled lightly with gold glitter and sprayed with a matte fixative. The window is trimmed with gold-border paper folded in half lengthwise so that it is glued down over the cut surface. The bottom of the inside of the egg is filled with hot whipped paraffin. The deer, tiny cone, and dried evergreen are pressed into the wax before it cools. Hang the egg with a loop of white velvet ribbon.

FIGURE 29 Winter scene in gold and white.

Ideas for Window Eggs — Special Occasions

Mother's Day Egg. Harden a large egg. Cut round windows around the egg, one for each child. Cut circular faces out of snapshots of the children and glue them into the windows. Trim around the windows with gold paper or gold braid. If the doors were removed intact, trim them, and glue or hinge them into place so that each one opens to reveal the picture underneath. To make a hinge small enough for these windows, cut a ½-inch length of transparent tape. Fold it over itself so that it is about ½ inch long and 1/8 inch wide. Bend it in the middle. Glue one end to the door and the other end to the shell. Conceal it under the trim.

Cut out pictures of flowers, and découpage them to the outside of each door and around the windows on the egg. Spray

FIGURE 30 Custard the Dragon.

By Mrs. F. R. Lawson

FIGURE 31 Window goose egg with two ceramic snails.

By Mrs. F. R. Lawson

the egg with several coats of clear lacquer. Make a pedestal by stacking several pearl collars on a daisy stand.

Graduation Egg. Cut a window in an egg. Make an easel from four pieces of balsa wood or matchsticks. Cut a picture of the graduate from a snapshot. Frame it with a gold-paper frame and glue it to the easel. Mount the picture and easel inside the egg. Complete the trim as desired. Make a stand by constructing a miniature mortarboard from black construction paper. Glue a circle of cardboard inside the mortarboard to make it sturdy enough to stand.

Wedding Egg. Cut a large oval from a double-yolk goose egg. Spray the outside silver. Découpage cutouts from wedding gift-wrap paper to the outside.   Use gold paper that has been silvered to complete the trim. Line the egg with lace left over from the wedding gown. Mount the figures from the wedding cake inside the egg. If these figures are too large, small bridal figures are available from bakeries and greeting-card stores. Cut two small plastic curtain rings so that they can be linked; link them, and glue them back together. Spray them gold. Use them to hang the egg or glue them in front of a pearl collar for a stand.

An Egg Valentine. Cut a heart-shaped window in the egg. Trim the edge of the opening with gathered ribbon-lace and red grosgrain ribbon. Mount a small plastic cupid inside the egg and complete the trim as desired.

Ideas for Window Eggs — Humorous

Custard the Dragon (Figure 30).   This goose egg was left white and a hanger was made with a loop of gold cord ringed with pearls. The outside of the egg was trimmed with three lengths of green grosgrain ribbon running from top to bottom. Glue rows of green sequins beside the ribbon. Space ½-inch green spangles between the ribbons and glue a pearl to each spangle. The rim of the oval window is trimmed with two rows of narrow, gold rickrack with a row of green sequins between them. The floor inside the egg is made by covering the top and sides of a piece of styrofoam with green felt and gluing it in the bottom of the egg. Glue a whimsical little green ceramic dragon on the felt. With forceps, glue a few pieces of dried weed and sea oat-heads so that they stand up like bushes around the dragon. Also see Plate 15.

Snails (Figure 31).   Cut a large oval window in a goose egg. Spray-paint both the inside and the outside with light yellow enamel. Thin burnt-sienna oil paint with turpentine and brush it on the egg with a cotton ball. Shade the color lightly from the base upward and from the edge of the window toward the back and sides. The shading effect matches the coloring on the ceramic snails. Trim the outside of the egg with gold braid and a loop of gold cord for a hanger. Inside the egg, glue two tiny ceramic snails on pieces of dried shelf mushroom. Using forceps, complete the landscape with small pieces of dried moss and twigs. Also see Plate 1.

Chipmunk (Figure 32). A ceramic chipmunk surrounded by dried plant material stands on a green felt base. With forceps, position the plant material behind the stand or stick it into small holes punctured in the felt. Secure it with glue. The tassel on this egg is a green velvet bow. The egg is done entirely in soft greens and browns that correspond to the colors of the chipmunk. Also see Plate 1.

Deer (Figure 33). The deer is a natural bisque figure surrounded by dried lichens and seeds in a double-yolk egg. The egg is painted gold and trimmed with gold braid.

Siamese Cat (Figure 34). This egg is finished with touches of blue which bring out the cat's blue eyes. Since the figurine suggested a creature that would be most at home in elegant surroundings, the egg was finished accordingly. (In contrast, the chipmunk and the deer suggested natural surroundings and muted colors. These eggs exemplify the need to consider the nature of the material when planning the entire window egg.) The outside of the egg in Figure 34 is appropriately trimmed with gold lace foil, blue braid, and Austrian cut rhinestones.

By Mrs. F. R. Lawson

FIGURE 32 Ceramic chipmunk in a window egg.

By Mrs. F. R. Lawson

FIGURE 34 Siamese cat in an elegant window egg.

By Mrs. F. R. Lawson

FIGURE 33 Bisque deer figurine in a window egg.

WINDOW EGGS

FIGURE 35 Delightful children's eggs.

The inside is finished with cutout pieces of the same foil, brocade, ballantine, and more rhinestones.

The Owl and the Pussy Cat (Figure 35). Paint an egg with an oval window inside and out with sky-blue acrylic paint. Make a hanger with a loop of light blue velvet ribbon glued around the egg. Line the inside of the egg with blue paraffin, allowing the paraffin to pool in the bottom of the egg to form the sea. Cut a moon and a star from lightweight cardboard and press them into the warm paraffin on the back of the egg. When the paraffin is partially set, press a green balsa-wood boat and a cardboard fish into the paraffin in the bottom of the shell. Stand the egg in a water glass to hold it in position until the paraffin cools. The owl and the cat are made from wooden beads and painted with acrylic paints. The cat's tail is a piece of wire glued to the body. The ears are paper. Glue a sail made from a piece of paper on a short length of wire to the boat. When the paraffin is dry, glue the cat and owl to the boat.

Many nursery tales such as "Little Bo-Peep" and "The Three Bears" can be recreated inside eggs. Use wooden beads for the central figures and trim the egg with cardboard cutouts to complete the story. Decorate the outside of the egg with cutout or painted nursery rhymes.

Mother Goose Egg (Figure 35). A Mother Goose is painted on the outside back of the shell and the egg is given a porcelain

FIGURE 36 Flower the Skunk.

FIGURE 37 The whimsical cat.

finish. Inside, the egg is left white. The goose stands on velvet and is surrounded by pieces of dried fern.

Girl with a Dog (Figure 35).   The antique figure of a girl with a dog is surrounded by cotton glued into the back of the egg. This egg has a spray of clay roses on the outside. Flowers and shell were given a porcelain finish.

Flower the Skunk (Figure 36 and Plate 13).   In this children's egg the skunk stands on green felt. Bright paper flowers are glued to the felt and to the inside back of the egg. The exterior is done in black and silver, the same colors as the skunk itself.

The Whimsical Cat (Figure 37 and Plate 13). The cat in this egg is a blue glass figure. Because the figure itself is clearly from the world of pretend, fanciful flowers were painted on construction paper, cut out and glued to flexible wire stems. The stems were glued into the piece of an egg carton on which the cat stands. The outside of the egg is bright blue, trimmed with red, white, and blue cotton braid.

More Window Egg Ideas

Glass Swan (Plate 5 and Figure 38).   The glass swan in a pale green, porcelain-finished goose egg stands on a piece of aluminum foil folded over styrofoam and glued into the base of the egg. The grass is Easter-basket cellophane. The interior has been ballantined.

FIGURE 38 Glass swan.

FIGURE 39   Jewelled lapel-pin owl.
By Mrs. F. R. Lawson

FIGURE 40   Bridesmaid egg.
By Mrs. F. R. Lawson

Jewelled Owl (Figure 39). This goose egg was painted emerald green with metal-flake paint. The outside of the egg is trimmed with gold cord and green sequins. It is hung with a loop of gold braid. The owl, a lapel pin trimmed with fake stones, is surrounded by pieces of dried pressed grass, mimosa leaf, and spore cases from sensitive fern. Also see Plate 1

Bridesmaid (Figure 40).   This egg is given several coats of pink pearlized nail polish on the outside. The rim of the window is decorated with pink braid, pearls, and tiny white artificial flowers. The inside of the egg is left white. A pink plastic bridesmaid is glued on a piece of styrofoam covered with white velour. Also see Plate 17.

Doll-House Egg.   A large egg is cut with square door and is trimmed on the outside to resemble a doll house. (See the Christmas house, Figure 26.) Tiny windows can be cut in both sides and given plastic-wrap panes. Glue on cardboard shutters. Paint the inside with acrylic paint. Make furniture out of lightweight cardboard. Tables and chairs with only two legs can be cut out of cardboard and glued to the shell. Paint the other two legs on the shell. Use this egg as the setting for very tiny, antique, doll-house furnishings or decorate it to resemble an old-fashioned store.

Flower-Arrangement Egg.   Design this egg to show off a tiny vase. Glue dried flowers into the vase and mount the vase inside the egg. Finish the egg with antique découpage papers and gold papers. Dry your own flowers in silica gel or purchase small dried flowers. Tiny artificial flowers are difficult to find but are very pretty. Instead of a vase, make the central object in the egg a floral spray of costume jewelry.

Peep-Show Egg.   The window in a peep-show egg is made by cutting off one end of the eggshell. These eggs resemble old-fashioned sugar eggs with a peep window. Lay the egg on its side and arrange a scene inside. Two-dimensional paper figures glued to lightweight cardboard can be used. Cut the cardboard so that a piece extends beyond the bottom of each figure. Bend this flap back and glue it to the egg. Paint additional parts of the scene on the inside back and sides of the shell. Because these eggs are deep, the perspective must be planned carefully. Insert the pieces with forceps.

Ideas for Special Cuts and Shapes

Reversed Window Egg.   Cut one or more oval windows from an egg. Reverse the cut pieces and glue them back into the openings they came from so that they make concave panels

FIGURE 41 Mermaid egg.

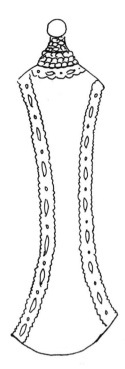

Ornament in an ornament egg.

instead of windows in the egg. Mount a figure or picture inside each concave panel. Three panels around an egg are very effective.

Ornament in an Ornament Egg. Cut two large ovals from an egg so that only the top and bottom and two slender arches remain. Reinforce the shell. Trim both edges inside and out. Jewel the arches remaining between the ovals. Suspend a glass Christmas ornament with nylon fishline inside the egg.

Mermaid Egg (Figure 41). Cut a goose egg in half lengthwise and paint the inside of both halves with several coats of pink pearlized nail polish. Use bronze model-paint on the outside halves. Make a stand from a round piece of wood or clay, 1½ inches in diameter by ½ inches thick. Paint it bronze. Mount the two shell halves by gluing them so that they stand open like a clam shell. Build up enough glue at the junction to hold them in place. Trim the inside edges with narrow pink ribbon and the outside with gold braid. Stand a small mermaid inside the shell; glue a large pearl and a piece of coral beside her. See Plate 16.

Piggy-bank egg.

Piggy-Bank Egg. With a grinding wheel mounted in a power drill, cut a slit in the top of a goose egg. Make the slot wide enough to accommodate small coins. Use beads or pearls for feet. Decorate as desired, but be sure to harden this egg.

FIGURE 42 Egg made into a small vase.

Easter-basket egg.

Vase Egg (Figure 42 and Plate 5).   Draw six scallops around a goose egg about an inch from the rounded end of the egg. Cut this section off with a razor blade and glue it to the other end of the egg to make a stand. Make a ring of gold paper and clip the edges on both sides. As you glue the two pieces of shell together, position the ring of paper at the junction. Paint the shell pale pink or mauve, and trim both cut edges with a narrow line of gold paint. Paint six gold lines from the scalloped edges to the gold paper at the base. With acrylic paint, draw nosegays or sprays of flowers in each of the six sections and give the egg a porcelainlike finish with glue and lacquer. To use this egg as a vase for fresh flowers, stand a pill bottle or a very small glass inside the egg to hold the water. Remember that water can soak through the shell and damage the finish on the egg.

Bell. Cut off the pointed end of an egg with a scalloped edge. Discard the small end, invert and decorate the bell as desired. Make a clapper from a large teardrop pearl or jewel. Suspend the pearl on a cord or fine chain from the top of the egg.

Easter Basket.   Cut an egg in half crosswise, discarding the pointed end. Trim the half shell with cut out Easter pictures. Trim the cut edge with braid. Make a handle with the same braid concealing the ends under the trim on the cut edge. Line the egg with Easter grass and fill it with small candy eggs. Make a May basket the same way.

Cradle Egg. (Figure 43). Cut out one quarter of a whole eggshell so that the remaining shell resembles a hooded cradle. Paint the egg pale pink or pale blue with acrylic paint. Spray it with gloss lacquer. Trim the outside edges with gathered ribbon lace and pink or blue velvet ribbon. Cut two rockers from cardboard and glue them to the egg. Line the cradle with fabric and place a tiny doll inside. If no doll is available, cut an oval of cardboard to fit inside the egg. Cover one side of the cardboard with fabric to look like a coverlet and make a tiny pillow by folding a small piece of the same fabric.

Boat Egg. Make a boat using half an eggshell. Make the mast from coat-hanger wire or a small dowel, and the sail from paper. Outfit the boat with tiny toy sailors, which are available in model shops, or devise your own from household scraps.

FIGURE 43 Party favor made from a hen's egg.

Landscape egg.

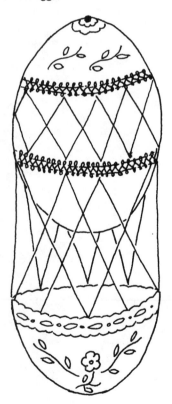

Balloon egg.

Balloon Egg. The balloon is fashioned from a whole egg and the gondola is made from an egg cut in half crosswise. Decorate with gold-cord guide wires, jewels, and gold découpage papers in a fanciful design.

Landscape Egg. Cut the egg crosswise. Build a platform of balsa wood or shirt cardboard in the bottom half, adjusting it so that the upper half will fit over it when the egg is closed. Decorate the platform with tiny figures available for N-gauge model trains.

6

FABULOUS EGGS

The advanced hobbyist will want to make eggs for special occasions and eggs reminiscent of the Imperial Russian Easter eggs. Christmas and Easter come to mind immediately when planning eggs as part of seasonal decorations, but eggs for Valentine's Day, Mother's Day, and birthdays are just as much fun. As we've seen, eggs can also be designed as part of a family event such as a wedding, graduation, or baby shower.

In making Fabergé-inspired eggs, you will want to use lavish amounts of gold paper, jewels, pearls, and velvet. Metallic paints, gold leaf, and a porcelainlike finish are most successful on these eggs, but discriminate between excessive use of jewels and pearls and artistic use of design and materials. Encrusting an egg with rows and rows of large rhinestones would be inappropriate for the delicacy of the material. While the Fabergé eggs are often elaborate, there is a basic simplicity in the choice and use of materials which is the hallmark of good design.

Because many of these eggs have complex and multiple cuts, a power tool is very helpful. Hand cutting must be done with a razor blade or a jeweler's file. Goose and duck eggs are much easier to work with than fragile hens' eggs, but any egg that is extensively cut should be reinforced or hardened.

You may want to try gold leaf and real gemstones on an egg. Large eggs may have an antique watch (Figure 52) or the

FIGURE 44 Egg in a gold-cord cage.

works from a music box mounted in them. These eggs can be the setting for a fine miniature painting (Figure 52) or a treasured antique. Gold charms from charm bracelets make nice accessories. Because eggs like these are works of art in their own right, they deserve a place of honor under a glass display dome. Remember to sign the eggs you are proud of.

Ideas for Fabulous Eggs

Egg in a Cage (Figure 44). Paint a whole, blown goose egg with purple metal-flake paint. Very lightly sketch guidelines on the egg with white chalk before gluing the gold cord in place. The cord is glued on in nine lines that begin at the top of the egg and spiral to the bottom in an S-curve. Finish the top with a large pearl and the bottom with a series of pearl collars.

Egg with Paintings. Découpage three or four circular paintings around an egg. Frame the paintings with gold paper and give the egg a porcelain finish. Trim the egg with velvet ribbon, a tassel of metallic cord, and a collar and jewel at the top. Hang the egg with a loop of nylon filament fishline. Select jewels and velvet which pick up the colors in the painting.

Pearl Egg. Paint a small egg a pastel shade or leave it white. After giving it a porcelainlike finish, stand it on a pearl collar and stud the entire egg with pearls, spaced ½ to ¾ inches apart, depending on the size of the egg. Connect the pearls with gold cord or paint on gold lines so that you have made an overall diamond pattern with a pearl at the points of each diamond.

Egg Surprise. Cut three eggs — a goose egg, an extra large hen's egg, and a pullet egg — in half crosswise. Decorate and line each egg in the same style but in three different colors. Make a pedestal for the goose egg. Nest the pullet egg inside the hen's egg and then nest the hen's egg inside the goose egg.

Display-Case Egg (Figure 45).   Draw three circles 1-1/8 inch in diameter around the egg, centering them just below the line of the equator. Draw a circle around the rounded end of the shell about one inch from the top. Before you begin to cut, reinforce the entire egg with transparent tape. Working slowly, cut all four circles with a razor blade. Do not cut completely through any section until they have all been partially cut. Remove the reinforcing tape, and reinforce the shell from the inside.

Cut the bottom quarter inch from three individual sections of an egg carton. Fit these inside the egg so that they form three bay windows behind the round openings. When you are certain they will fit, remove them. Coat them with glue and line them with a soft, drapeable black fabric. Let them dry. Line the inside of the top piece of the eggshell in the same way.

Replace the egg carton pieces inside the egg and secure them with transparent tape. Cut a round piece of lightweight cardboard to fit in the top of the egg so that it rests on the egg carton sections. Make a cardboard ring to fit between the circle and the edge of the shell. Cover both pieces. While they dry, glue a small brass hinge to the top lid and the main shell, slipping it between the egg-carton sections. Glue the covered cardboard circle and ring in place inside the top of the egg. Use gold paper to trim the outside of the round windows, the inside and outside of the lid, and the outside cut edge of the shell.

Make a pedestal from a long, tapered lid of a nail polish bottle and gild it with gold leaf. Cover a piece of wood with the black fabric that you used before. Cut a circle of cardboard and glue it over the fabric on the bottom of the piece of wood. Glue the nail-polish cap to the egg and to the stand.

Mask the fabric and spray the egg with gloss lacquer. Jewel as desired. Glue the small items to be displayed into the three windows and onto the fabric in the top.

This same design can be modified to make an egg that will hold an antique watch or music box in the top section. Cutout pictures can be glued in the lower windows, or the round sections which are removed from the lower windows can be reversed and glued back into the shell to make concave areas to be jeweled. When using this design to hold a watch, secure the watch in the top section instead of lining the top. Omit the cardboard egg-carton sections, and decorate the three windows with pictures.

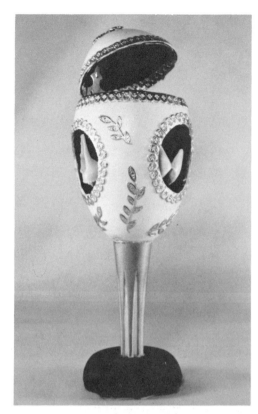

FIGURE 45 A goose egg with multiple windows.

Empire Egg (Figure 46 and Plate 14). This goose egg is easy to make and makes a spectacular effect. The stand is made by gluing a wooden ring and a wooden bead together on a decorative plastic door plaque. All three items can be found in hardware stores. Select a large, blemish-free goose egg. Divide the egg into thirds and lightly sketch on the pattern with a hard pencil. This egg uses deep rose velvet and light rose rhinestones. The braid and cord are gold. Silver bugles and tiny white pearls complete the design.

Gold-Leafed Eggs. The eggs in Figures 47-52 and Plates 9, 15, 19, and 21-23 (except the center egg in Figure 47) have all been gold-leafed with Hasting's 24-karat gold leaf (see page 46). Nos. 4 and 6 rhinestones and pearls from Jewel Creations were used in the decoration. Since it is impossible to make pencil marks on gold leaf, make a scale drawing or cut a template from shirt cardboard to help position the rows of stones evenly

FIGURE 46 Empire egg.

FIGURE 47 Circus egg with one door open.   By Mary Sammartino

By Mary Sammartino

FIGURE 48 Circus egg, doors closed.

around the egg. A dressmaker's tape is also useful. Apply the glue to the egg with a hatpin, being very careful not to get any on the face of the stones. Position the rhinestones with a piece of jeweler's wax on a hatpin.

The stands in Figures 51-53, and Plate 19 are made from pieces of lamps or from small, inexpensive figurines that have been gold-leafed. Additional rhinestones and pearls are glued onto the stands. The inside of most of these eggs is finished with Hasting's white gold-leaf.

Circus Egg (Figures 47 and 48). This goose egg was cut with a jeweler's file. The latch, hinges, wheels, carriage assembly, umbrella, and carousel were cut from the metal top of a juice can and gold-leafed. The outside of the egg is Hasting's 24-karat gold leaf. The inside is Hasting's white gold-leaf. The wheel assembly is mounted with a fine-wire axle so that it rolls and turns. The carousel is mounted with a shaft on a pin so that it rotates. The interior figures are from charm bracelets. The egg is jewelled with Nos. 4 and 6 ruby and crystal rhinestones and pearls. Also see Plate 23.

Carriage Egg (Figure 49 and Plate 9). This goose egg was cut in the same way as the circus egg in Figures 47 and 48, and

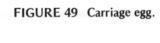

By Mary Sammartino

FIGURE 49 Carriage egg.

FIGURE 50 Watch egg, French ring box, and gold-leafed egg
with a painting of St. John and the Christ child.

By Mary Sammartino

By Mary Sammartino

FIGURE 51 Interior of the egg shown in
Plate 19.

finished in yellow and white gold-leaf. The coach is a souvenir copy of Queen Elizabeth's coronation coach. It rotates on a pin shaft and stands on a piece of metal cut from a coffee can painted red. The stand is one sold at rock shops for mounting mineral specimens. Note the fine gold chain holding the lid, which opens on a handmade hinge. The egg is decorated with fine gold cord, and 6 crystal and ruby rhinestones. The top is made by mounting a crystal from a watch face on a double circle of gold cord. Under the watch face, the date is formed in very tiny pearls.

Three Fabulous Eggs (Figure 50). In the hen's egg on the left, the door is made from a small watch. This egg was gold-leafed and jewelled. The center egg is painted with white enamel. The egg is trimmed with rows of red crystal rocailles, gold cord, and pearls. It opens to reveal cutouts of gold découpage papers glued in a decorative pattern on the white shell. The egg on the right is a glassine egg, but the technique used is equally

GETTING STARTED IN EGG DECORATION

FIGURE 52 Watch egg and miniature painting on a stand that fits inside the egg.

By Mary Sammartino

FIGURE 53   Diamond-studded egg.

By Mary Sammartino

successful on real eggshell. Gold-leaf the egg. Cut an oval from an Italian silk and glue it in place with white glue. Conceal the edge of the silk with gold cord. The egg can be hung from the fine gold chain attached to an earring finding that is glued to the top of the egg.

Angel Egg (Figure 51 and Plate 19).   Both illustrations show the same egg. In Plate 19 the painted porcelain oval glued to the shell door is closed. In Figure 51 the door is opened to reveal a gold-leafed angel ringing a bell inside the egg.

Watch Egg (Figure 52). In this egg a door on the reverse side opens, allowing the removal of the tiny stand that holds a miniature painting. The watch is mounted in a bracket of soft metal and can be removed to be wound.

Diamond-studded Egg (Figure 53). This dark blue enamelled goose egg stands on part of a lamp base which has been gold-leafed and jewelled. It opens to show an ivory bust of David mounted within.

SUPPLIERS

American Handicrafts, a subsidiary of the Tandy Corporation, has stores in many large cities. Their catalog lists many of the same materials as those offered by Delco. For their address, consult your phone directory.

Delco Craft Center, Inc., 30081 Stephenson Highway, Madison Heights, Mich. 48017
    acrylic paints; balsa wood; beads; brass hardware; brushes; butterflies; chalks; glue; lacquer; Moto tools; rhinestones; round beads; Rub 'n Buff; sequins; spray fixative; utility knives; varnish; wooden figures

Jewel Creations, 38 W. 31st Street, New York, N. Y. 10001 (Stores also in other major cities.)
    cameos; gold chains; painted ovals; pearls; rhinestones (small, fine quality)

National Art Craft Supply Co., 12213 Euclid Avenue, Cleveland, Ohio 44106
    filigree caps; findings; tools

Sy Schweitzer and Co., Inc., P. O. Box 61, Gedney Station, White Plains, N. Y. 10605
    filigree, findings

Surma Book and Music Co., 11 E. 7th Street, New York, N.Y. 10003
   Supplies and directions for making Ukrainian eggs.

Taylor House, Bench and Ferry Streets, Galena, Ill. 61036
   antique papers; braids; bugles; collars; découpage papers; figures (small); jewels; rocailles, sequins, etc. Taylor House also puts out a newsletter for egg hobbyists that gives suggestions and drawings for decorating eggs.

Lee Ward's, Elgin, Ill. 60120
   boutiquing items

INDEX